TIME LIFE BOOKS ®

The Time-Life Library of Boating
Human Behavior
The Art of Sewing
The Old West
The Emergence of Man
The American Wilderness
The Time-Life Encyclopedia of Gardening
Life Library of Photography
This Fabulous Century
Foods of the World
Time-Life Library of America
Time-Life Library of Art
Great Ages of Man
Life Science Library
The Life History of the United States
Time Reading Program
Life Nature Library
Life World Library
Family Library:
   How Things Work in Your Home
   The Time-Life Book of the Family Car
   The Time-Life Family Legal Guide
   The Time-Life Book of Family Finance

LIFE LIBRARY OF PHOTOGRAPHY

The Studio

BY THE EDITORS OF TIME-LIFE BOOKS

TIME-LIFE BOOKS, NEW YORK

ON THE COVER: Some basic equipment used by a professional studio photographer—flood and spot lamps at left, and a 4 x 5 view camera at right. The ground-glass viewing screen of the camera shows the inverted image of a still life—chessmen on a board—arranged on seamless paper and illuminated by the spot and the flood.

Contents

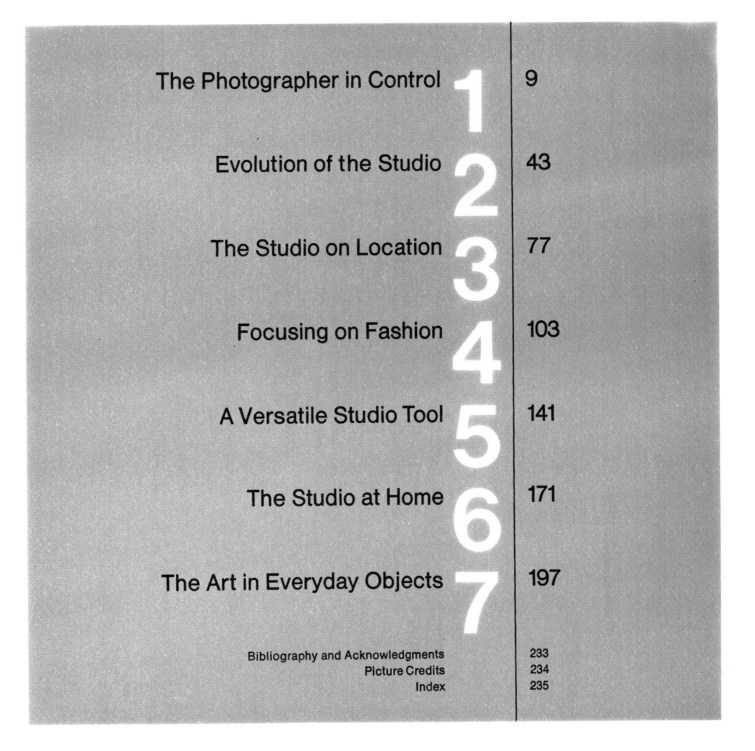

The Photographer in Control **1** 9

Evolution of the Studio **2** 43

The Studio on Location **3** 77

Focusing on Fashion **4** 103

A Versatile Studio Tool **5** 141

The Studio at Home **6** 171

The Art in Everyday Objects **7** 197

Bibliography and Acknowledgments 233
Picture Credits 234
Index 235

TIME-LIFE BOOKS

FOUNDER: Henry R. Luce 1898-1967

Editor-in-Chief: Hedley Donovan
Chairman of the Board: Andrew Heiskell
President: James R. Shepley

Vice Chairman: Roy E. Larsen

MANAGING EDITOR: Jerry Korn
Assistant Managing Editors: Ezra Bowen,
David Maness, Martin Mann, A. B. C. Whipple
Planning Director: Oliver E. Allen
Art Director: Sheldon Cotler
Chief of Research: Beatrice T. Dobie
Director of Photography: Melvin L. Scott
Senior Text Editors: Diana Hirsh, William Frankel
Assistant Planning Director: Carlotta Kerwin
Assistant Art Director: Arnold C. Holeywell
Assistant Chief of Research: Myra Mangan

PUBLISHER: Joan D. Manley
General Manager: John D. McSweeney
Business Manager: John Steven Maxwell
Sales Director: Carl G. Jaeger
Promotion Director: Paul R. Stewart
Public Relations Director: Nicholas Benton

LIFE LIBRARY OF PHOTOGRAPHY

Editorial Staff for *The Studio:*
EDITOR: Robert G. Mason
Picture Editor: Simone Daro Gossner
Text Editor: Jay Brennan
Designer: Raymond Ripper
Assistant Designer: Herbert H. Quarmby
Staff Writers: Maitland A. Edey, Paula Pierce,
Suzanne Seixas, John von Hartz, Bryce S. Walker
Chief Researcher: Peggy Bushong
Researchers: Kathleen Brandes, Malabar Brodeur,
Helen Greenway, Monica O. Horne,
Nancy Jacobsen, Myra Mangan, Shirley Miller,
Don Nelson, Jane Sugden, Johanna Zacharias
Art Assistant: Patricia Byrne

Editorial Production
Production Editor: Douglas B. Graham
Assistant Production Editors:
Gennaro C. Esposito, Feliciano Madrid
Quality Director: Robert L. Young
Assistant Quality Director: James J. Cox
Associate: Serafino J. Cambareri
Copy Staff: Eleanore W. Karsten (chief),
Barbara Quarmby, Ruth Kelton, Florence Keith,
Pearl Sverdlin
Picture Department: Dolores A. Littles
Traffic: Carmen McLellan

Portions of this book were written by Edmund
White. Valuable aid also was contributed by the
following departments and individuals of Time
Inc.: TIME-LIFE Photo Lab, George Karas, Herbert
Orth; Editorial Production, Norman Airey; Library,
Benjamin Lightman; Picture Collection, Doris
O'Neil; TIME-LIFE News Service, Murray J. Gart;
Correspondents Elisabeth Kraemer (Bonn),
Margot Hapgood (London), Maria Vincenza Aloisi
(Paris), Ann Natanson (Rome) and Sungyung
Chang (Tokyo).

Photography can be approached from either of two directions. One approach is the way of the photojournalist, the quick-eyed observer who catches life on the wing as it flies past the camera lens, capturing the spontaneous picture that will make the front page—or the family album.

The studio photographer travels an entirely different route. A painstaking craftsman, he plans a picture as carefully as an architect designs a house, often taking days to arrange his composition and adjust his lighting before clicking his shutter. Rather than reporting events from the sidelines, he stages his own and exercises total control.

To acquire this control and increase his flexibility, the amateur beginning studio photography may wish to acquire a whole roomful of paraphernalia —floodlights, spotlights, reflectors, tripods, electronic-flash units and view cameras of various sizes. He may also wish, as professionals do, to operate like the designer of a theatrical production, constructing entire sets. Professional studios are sometimes large and elaborate, with barn-sized rooms, carloads of expensive equipment and big staffs of photo assistants, set builders, wardrobe mistresses and stylists. But an expensive establishment is really unnecessary for most studio work, and any amateur can set up his own studio with nothing more than a camera, a room, a few lights, and perhaps a roll of seamless photographic paper for a backdrop. And by borrowing a few techniques from professionals, he can even come close to their goal: a kind of photographic perfection reachable only through the studio photographer's unique ability to manipulate every step of the picture-taking process.

The Editors

The Photographer in Control 1

Making, Not Taking, Pictures 12

The Craft of Portraiture 20
Fashions Indoors and Out 30
The Portrait of a Pet 32
Catching the Charm of a Child 34
Art for Advertising's Sake 36

Three of the 34 great-grandchildren of the distinguished American architect Stanford White pose in period clothes in an ornate hall of White's Long Island estate. The comfort of the familiar house and the fun of trying on costumes enabled the children to radiate the sense of leasure that infuses the picture, which was made in sunlight bounced from an adjoining porch.

TONI FRISSELL: *Costume Trunk*, 1964

Art for Advertising's Sake

MILTON HALBERSTADT: *Still Life with Tomatoes, 1962*

The making of an expert still life demands close adherence to the basic rules of studio photography: pay keen attention to detail, arrange objects with concern for composition and, above all, take maximum pains with lighting.

Since most still lifes are now made for commercial purposes, they challenge the studio photographer to find esthetic values in the humblest of utilitarian objects *(left).* But sometimes a commercial assignment inspires art for art's sake. The picture on the opposite page was the result of a sudden inspiration that came to photographer Nob Fukuda in his Osaka studio while he was making some photographs of small kitchen appliances. He removed them from his table and replaced them with these items: a framed reproduction of a painting by the 19th Century French artist Henri Rousseau, several hemp palm leaves in a vase and four eggs. Given the proper lighting, the ingredients formed a still life of simple dignity.

This still life, made as an advertisement for tomato paste, shows a halved tomato near a bell jar containing other pieces of the fruit. In the background is a jar of water with sprigs of fennel, an herb used in making the paste. Light comes from a specially designed fixture—a 10-foot-high parabolic apparatus using five bulbs of 500 watts each—that shows the succulence of the fruit.

To bring out the interplay of light, shadow and ▶ color in this serene still life, three light sources were used. One 500-watt bulb was placed in the overhead fixture. Another 500-watt bulb went into a flood lamp on the right, diffused through translucent paper. A 1,000-watt spot was played on the table to convey the shape of the eggs.

NOB FUKUDA: *Still Life*, 1970

In the 19th Century commercial enterprises relied entirely on art work for their advertisements and promotional publications. Today they go primarily to the studio photographer, whose camera is used to stimulate buyer interest in everything from sewing accessories *(opposite)* to automobiles *(overleaf)*.

Often the public attitude toward a product or service—the image, both literal and figurative—is determined by photographs. Indeed, photographers are sometimes called in as consultants when a new line is to be promoted. This was the case when Love Cosmetics decided to market some of its products in futuristic package designs. The photographer, Henry Sandbank, worked closely with the packaging designer and advertising art director as they developed a cosmetic line that would appeal to young women who grew up in the space age. Sandbank then created a series of pictures, one of which is at left, emphasizing the glistening metallic look of the new products.

The cylindrical, modernistic cast of these cosmetics containers was emphasized by placing them on a large sheet of Plexiglass and lighting from below with two 500-watt floodlights. A 750-watt spotlight trained on them from above introduced highlights on the burnished surfaces.

To emphasize the slate coloring of the zipper ▶ and seam binding in this advertising picture for sewing accessories, Peter Scolamiero bought a piece of slate and spread the articles on it. To soften the picture, he employed two 1,000-watt lights diffused through a sheet of opal glass.

HENRY SANDBANK: *Cosmetics Containers,* 1968

PETER SCOLAMIERO: *Notions on Slate*, 1968

Studio photographers, along with automobile stylists, long ago began capitalizing on the fact that to many people a car is more than a means of transportation; it is also a status symbol, a member of the family—and a functional triumph of modern technology. The photographers' job was to heighten this complex of feelings, thus increasing pride of ownership—and sales. As a result, automobiles have been photographed in every exotic—and familiar —corner of the globe.

Ernst Haas took his handsome mood shot for Volkswagen using an adobe church in New Mexico as a backdrop connoting strength and durability *(left);* Hiro, on location in California *(opposite),* viewed the Mercury as a machine with a unique place of its own in society —and he decided to make a portrait, not merely a picture. To convey the sense of life, he strategically placed three lights: one in the interior to "wake it up," another under the front grill "to lift it off the ground," and the third aimed at the front to bring out the contours. He also opened the doors, suggesting that the automobile possesses wings or even open arms. ☐

The photographer was in Taos, New Mexico, when this picture came to him. With the sun's rays casting a shadow of the car on the adobe wall of a church, he composed his photograph to relate a durable product of mass production to an example of timeless craftsmanship.

For this new-model portrait of a metallic brown ▶ sedan, Hiro placed the automobile on a promontory at Big Sur, California. Shooting on a hazy mid-morning with strobe lights and infrared film, he experimented with some 20 different combinations of filters, putting three and four of them onto his camera at a time, until he achieved this unusual vision of sleek, animated power.

ERNST HAAS: *Volkswagen in New Mexico, 1964*

HIRO: *Mercury at Big Sur,* 1970

When Burlington Industries asked Lionel
Freedman for a picture that would show all
the company's fabrics at once, he went to work on
this room setting in his large New York studio
(pages 64-67). No real room would ever contain
such a wide range of fabrics, so he decided
to build a surreal room of his own imagining. He
gave the picture a dreamlike quality by using
indirect lighting and by draping long strips from
bolts of cloth across the highly polished
floor. At the sides of the room, fabrics are
gathered in hangings, as a utilitarian
counterpoint to the wandering strips at center.

LIONEL FREEDMAN: *Fabric Display,* 1960

Evolution of the Studio 2

Techniques Past and Present 46

A 19th Century Portrait Parlor 48

Tintypes on Short Order 50

Splendor in the Big City 52

Tricks of the Trade from Hollywood 54

Pictures for the Sunday Millions 58

Fine Points of Food Photography 60

Producing Settings on Demand 64

Snow Scenes in July 68

Room for Rent 70

A thriving 19th Century studio, the establishment ►
of Henry Holler in Brooklyn, New York, is shown
opposite in an 1891 engraving. Used as a
trademark, it was printed on cardboard mountings
that the studio supplied with its pictures. The
large radial sign, oversized wall lettering and the
prideful claim to being an "art gallery" all
indicate the imposing place the photographic
studio had in the commercial life of the city.

Techniques Past and Present

From the very beginning, photography has been a studio art. The oldest surviving daguerreotype, made by Louis Daguerre in 1837, is a still life with plaster cupids and a wine bottle artfully arranged in a corner of the inventor's studio. An impressionistic murkiness pervades the picture, the result of dim interior lighting and the slow reaction time of the first cameras and plates. Nonetheless it is an admirable example of studio photography.

One of the first to be impressed was the American inventor Samuel F. B. Morse. He met Daguerre in Paris in 1839 and was so enthralled by the Frenchman's studio interiors that he declared them to be "Rembrandt perfected." He resolved to bring Daguerre's process to America, and in doing so, opened up one of this country's first photography studios.

Morse's principal interest was in making portraits. Besides being the inventor of the telegraph, he was one of the nation's leading portrait painters, and professor of art at New York University. Photography fascinated him because it promised to be a fast and accurate way to make portrait studies for his canvases. With a chemistry professor at N.Y.U., John W. Draper, who was interested in the scientific problems of photography, Morse built a glassed-in studio on the roof of the university building in 1840. Shortly afterward he opened a second studio, a veritable "palace for the sun," on the top floor of a nearby commercial building, and went into business, taking daguerreotype portraits and teaching photography, while waiting for the United States government to grant him recognition and money for his telegraph.

Like Morse, almost all the early studio photographers were portraitists. And all of them faced the same perplexing problem: how to bring enough light into the studio to make an exposure. Indoor exposure times for the early daguerreotypes were so protracted—a half hour or more—that portrait photography seemed at first impossible. How could any sitter keep still for so long a period? Daguerre himself said it could never be done, but inventive photographers were already working out ways to reduce exposure times by using faster lenses and concentrated light sources. Strong light, in fact, was a prerequisite. Most portrait photographers, like Morse, solved the lighting problem by building studios with glass roofs and directing the exterior light onto the subject's face with mirrors. There were some ingenious variations on this basic scheme. Alexander S. Wolcott, who opened a studio on New York's Broadway in March 1840, several months before Morse opened his, brought in sunlight through the window. He used a system of gigantic reflectors cantilevered over the sidewalk to catch the sun's rays and focus them onto the subject. To protect the sitter's eyes from glare, the light was filtered through a rack of glass bottles filled with blue dye.

Daguerreotype portrait studios were an immediate popular success. Everyone wanted his features immortalized by this miraculous new process.

"Daguerrean galleries," as they were called, sprang up in every city. By 1853 there were 86 in New York City alone, and an estimated 1,000 New Yorkers made their living by working in them. The Commonwealth of Massachusetts reported in 1855 that it had 134 professional daguerreotype artists, and that during the year they had made 403,626 pictures. The studios ranged from rudimentary to lavish. In frontier communities in the West, the local photographer might set up his camera in a single room over the barber shop. Some big-city daguerreotype studios were as richly appointed as opera houses, with commodious waiting rooms, an abundance of side rooms where the portraits were taken and labs where they were developed. One of the most fashionable was opened by Mathew B. Brady, later of Civil War fame, in New York in 1853. It profoundly impressed the reporter from Humphrey's *Daguerrean Journal,* who wrote: "The walls are covered with satin and gold paper. The ceiling frescoed, and in the center is suspended a six-light gilt and enamelled chandelier. . . . The golden cornices and festooned damasks indicate that Art dictated their arrangement."

Whether modest or magnificent, all the early studios shared some basic similarities. Usually they were installed on the building's top floor, with a skylight to bring daylight indoors. The subject ordinarily sat in a chair facing squarely into the camera, which was set on a tripod. To keep his head steady during exposure, he held it against a heavy wrought-iron stand with a headrest complete with clamp at the top. An adjustable mirror filled in the shadowed side of his face. Behind him was a plain cloth backdrop.

In the late 1850s the discovery of the more sensitive wet-plate, positive-negative system of photography simplified the lighting problem, but not studio décor. The simple tan or gray backdrops of earlier decades gave way to lavish painted canvases, depicting lush gardens with grapevines twining over Grecian columns, or to fancy interiors with paneled walls, staircases and marble statuary. The single chair was increased to a roomful of plush ottomans flanked by tables and balustrades, against which the subject would posture imperiously or loll seductively, depending on mood and sex.

Until well into the 20th Century, studio photography continued to mean portrait photography. But in the 1920s, the character of professional studios began to change. The increasing use of photographs in advertising meant that studios began to cater to the needs of industrial firms and fashion houses. Portrait studios remained, of course, making everything from passport photos to wedding pictures. But most of the big new studios adapted their operation to the needs of commercial clients. Some concentrated on fashion or furniture or food, some on photographing automobiles or heavy machinery. And so the major studios remain today—specialized, technically sophisticated purveyors of images to commerce and industry.

A 19th Century Portrait Parlor

◄ A 19th Century elegance characterizes a semi-restoration of Peter Britt's Photo Gallery in Jacksonville, Oregon, with its painted canvas backdrops, two posing chairs and various props, including a flight of steps, a stuffed egret and an urn on a curved pedestal. Behind the view camera on its tripod are two wrought-iron headrests.

Boxlike wooden view cameras (above left) were brought to Oregon from supply houses in San Francisco. One lens, with its heavy brass casing, weighed 30 pounds. Besides being a photographer, Britt was a skilled portrait painter, and examples of his art, with works by others, share the walls with his photographs. In the picture at right, above, a posing chair has been arranged against a backdrop to suggest palatial grandeur. The hole in the chair was needed for photographing babies. The mother would kneel out of sight behind the chair and hold the baby through the hole.

In Victorian America, every town worth its name boasted a photography studio. The local photographer was both resident portraitist and chronicler of town life. Every self-respecting citizen would sit importantly for his picture. Brides would pose in their wedding dresses, and young married couples would bring their first baby. On request, the photographer would lug his view cámera outside for a shot on location. He would pose the fire department beside its hook and ladder, the dry-goods merchant next to his calicoes and denims, and a family in front of its new house.

The photographer of Jacksonville, Oregon, Peter Britt, arrived in town in 1852, one year after a gold strike had sent the town booming. Trained as both a portrait painter and a photographer, he set up shop with a single box camera in a log cabin he built himself. Soon people from all over southern Oregon were flocking to his studio—miners celebrating a strike, bankers in top hats, Indians, soldiers, and settlers with their families. Britt expanded to new quarters, equipped with the elegant props shown here, which are now preserved in the Jacksonville Museum.

Tintypes on Short Order

As photographic portrait galleries grew ever more lavish—and more expensive—a new kind of studio emerged that catered to the taste and pocketbook of the workingman. It was devoted exclusively to producing portraits on tintype, a fast, cheap cousin of the daguerreotype, in which the photograph was made directly on a dark metal plate that had been coated with a light-sensitive emulsion. Because of the dark metallic background, the developed picture gave the illusion of being a positive rather than a negative. Like modern Polaroid instant pictures, tintypes could be taken, developed and handed over to the customer in a matter of minutes.

Tintype studios persisted until well into the 1930s, before succumbing to the more sophisticated camera techniques of modern times. But at least one still exists. At the Henry Ford Museum in Greenfield Village, a town reconstructed from America's past in Dearborn, Michigan, the tintype studio shown here has been set up in a small frame house. The visitor may still pose in front of the tintype camera like his grandfather before him, and have his image recorded for posterity on tin.

Tintype studios, like this reconstruction at Greenfield Village, were simple and functional. A monochrome background drapery hangs behind the posing chairs, an abbreviated armchair stands in the center, and a stool with a headrest is at right. The camera with its viewing cloth rests on a tripod in the center, and extra iron headrests are clustered along the left wall. A glass roof and floor-to-ceiling window admit daylight.

Tintype cameras, like the one at left, above, often had multiple lenses for taking several pictures at once. Since tintypes could not be printed, the only way to get a copy of a picture was to make another exposure. After the tintypes were snapped, they were developed and hung out to dry on stands like the ones at left. The entire process, from plate preparation and exposure to final portrait, took only five to ten minutes.

Splendor in the Big City

T. C. MARCEAU: *Portrait of a Lady*, date unknown

One of the most sumptuous of all the late-Victorian portrait studios was a gallery opened in New York City at the turn of the century. The studio's proprietor was a retired army officer, Colonel Theodore C. Marceau, who had already established a string of fashionable photo studios in Cincinnati, Los Angeles and San Francisco. In moving to the nation's largest city, Marceau resolved to outdo himself, and his competitors, in stylish extravagance. Although most of the city's portrait galleries were located in low-rent lofts along Broadway, Marceau splurged on a ground-floor storefront on Fifth Avenue. He then spent on furnishings and equipment what a photography journal of the day called "an amount unheard of in the establishment of photo studios." There were reception chambers and waiting rooms, and a special dressing room with an ornate marble make-up table where ladies could change into their best lace and damask evening gowns before posing decorously *(left)* in front of the camera. A fad for Middle Eastern art was currently sweeping New York society, and Marceau embellished his waiting room with Turkish draperies, carpets and ottomans.

Competing photographers scoffed at Marceau's presumption and prophesied his speedy bankruptcy. Marceau, however, not only survived, but captured a large part of the carriage trade. The bulk of his business resulted from a practice followed by fashionable ladies: they gave away framed pictures of themselves as Christmas presents. The number of sittings might rise to as many as 50 a day between Thanksgiving and Christmas. The customer would be ushered first to a dressing room to arrange her gown and hair, and then to a studio roughly 25 feet square and workmanlike in appearance, with camera, skylight or flood lamps, and the usual posing chairs and painted background panels. The photographer would take four or five different poses, and the customer would return a day or so later to choose the one she liked best. Marceau's prices were high—as much as $20 for one sitting and a dozen 5 x 7 sepia prints. But to a style-conscious society, nothing would do but a portrait from the city's fanciest gallery.

The street entrance to Colonel T. C. Marceau's ▶ posh Fifth Avenue photo gallery, with its window display of portraits in gold frames (top left), only hinted at the opulence inside. In addition to the ground-floor office and showroom (top right), there were a luxurious ladies' dressing room (bottom left), a waiting room done up to resemble a Turkish harem (bottom right) and several stories of light studios, workshops and darkrooms.

Tricks of the Trade from Hollywood

Simple or lavish, the Victorian studios never moved beyond the production of stylized portraits. But in the early 1900s a new national obsession—motion pictures—began to work dramatic changes in both the subject matter and the techniques of studio photography.

The movies seemed at first an unlikely source of photographic expertise. The earliest ones were murky one-reel shorts that flickered uneasily for five or ten minutes before expiring. They were shot in flat natural light, usually in jerry-built, open-air studios. But as directors grew more skilled, they began dressing up their product with lighting techniques, set designs and stage effects borrowed from the Broadway theater. Eventually these innovations, perfected on movie lots in Hollywood and on the East Coast, became part of the standard vocabulary of studios everywhere.

Increased realism in set design was the movies' first big contribution to studio techniques. The Jesse Lasky Feature Play Company, which from 1913 to 1915 made film adaptations of Broadway hits (above), used sets as detailed and convincing as any found behind a theater's proscenium. Innovations in lighting had to wait until the development of flood lamps. Lasky usually filmed in bright sunshine, building his sets out of doors on his Hollywood lot. Even when movie companies went inside, they splurged on huge greenhouses with glass roofs to let in the sun—like the Lubin Studio in Philadelphia (opposite), which was apparently light enough and large enough to stage three different scenes at once.

Learning to use the flood lamp was the movies' single most important breakthrough in studio techniques. It freed photographers from the flat, monotonous illumination that usually results from relying exclusively on daylight and opened up endless possibilities for creating dramatic effects.

Hollywood studios were surprisingly slow in converting to artificial light. Though the inventive Billy Bitzer, cameraman for the famous director D. W. Griffith, had used electric lighting as early as 1899—rigging some 400 arc lamps to film the Jeffries-Sharkey boxing match in New York City—Hollywood stayed with natural light until well after 1910. The main reason was economic. Sunshine was free, and in the halcyon climate of Southern California it hardly ever stopped for bad weather. But in 1915, Cecil B. De Mille began trying to duplicate the dramatic lighting effects he had learned while working at the Belasco Theater on Broadway.

De Mille first used velvet draperies and metallic reflectors to shade and direct the sunlight, but quickly switched to arc flood lamps. The results were moody and dramatic, and some scenes were so dim that De Mille's producer, Samuel Goldwyn, complained that "you couldn't see the actors' faces half the time." De Mille retorted by calling his new technique "Rembrandt lighting," which inspired Goldwyn to jack up the price of his films to movie houses. But the new lighting techniques did indeed provide an artistic and emotional impact that would have been impossible with natural light. They also gave cameramen the kind of control over their subject—even in uniformly illuminated scenes such as the one opposite—that has been an indispensable part of studio photography ever since.

Batteries of carbon-arc floodlights, some hung overhead, others mounted on standards at the sides—illuminate this early movie studio's vision of pandemonium on the New York Stock Exchange. Both for long shots and for dramatically lighted close-ups, artificial light allowed a versatility unmatched by older methods.

Pictures for the Sunday Millions

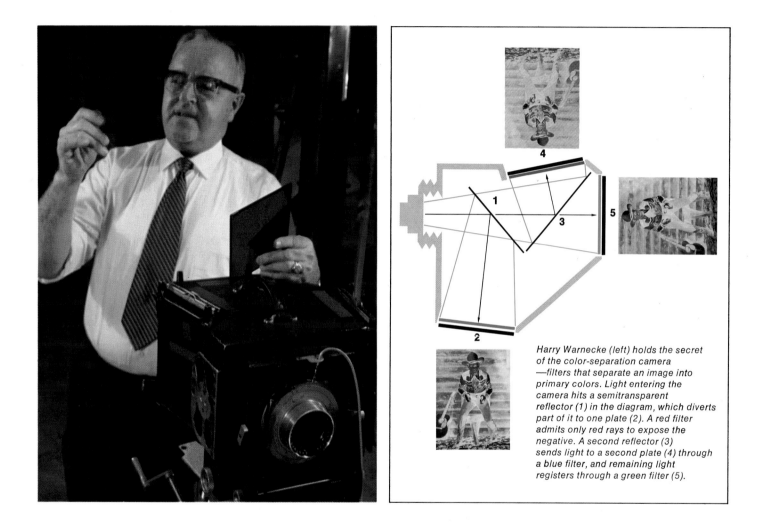

Harry Warnecke (left) holds the secret of the color-separation camera —filters that separate an image into primary colors. Light entering the camera hits a semitransparent reflector (1) in the diagram, which diverts part of it to one plate (2). A red filter admits only red rays to expose the negative. A second reflector (3) sends light to a second plate (4) through a blue filter, and remaining light registers through a green filter (5).

One of the first studios set up specifically for color photography was, paradoxically, established by a newspaper at a time when modern color film was still to be invented and ordinary newspaper letterpresses did not reproduce color photos satisfactorily. The driving force behind the idea was Harry Warnecke *(above)* a staff photographer for the New York *Daily News,* who had been experimenting with color on his own. He knew that color could be reproduced with the rotogravure printing process, which the *News* was already using to put out a Sunday picture section that included color advertisements. He convinced his bosses that a cover photograph in full color would be a worthwhile attraction.

The *News* backed Warnecke generously. He even designed a camera of his own—a big "one-shot" device *(diagramed above)* that simultaneously exposed three plates with black-and-white emulsion through three separate filters to make red, blue and green separations required for color reproduction. Using this and other specialized gear, Warnecke provided a steady supply of color pictures. And long before color snapshots were common, bathing beauties and movie stars *(opposite)* appeared in color in the *Sunday News.*

Hundreds of celebrities had their pictures snapped by Harry Warnecke's color-separation camera in the New York Daily News color studio (left), where the photographer himself adjusts the cranelike tripod that holds his bulky camera. The log cabin backdrop at the rear lent verisimilitude to the portrait of cowboy star Roy Rogers, taken in 1943. Photographers at the News studio built their own sets and created their own special effects, including a "snowstorm" of untoasted corn flakes sprinkled from a hand-cranked drum.

Fine Points of Food Photography

With new advances in lighting techniques, color and set design, studio photography had, by the 1950s, arrived at a versatility unimaginable to the early portraitists. Drawing from an increasingly sophisticated bag of photographic tricks, studio photographers gained the ability to conjure up a seemingly endless variety of special effects. They also acquired an entirely new breed of client—big business. Most large studios today work for large corporations, creating illustrations for magazine and book publishers and turning out photos for advertising agencies. This in turn has resulted in a new kind of specialization to meet the needs of commercial clients.

One of today's most important studio specialties is food photography. More money is spent advertising foods and beverages than any other kind of product—between $3 and $4 billion per year in the mid-1970s. Food photography is thus the main business of many studios, which must have special kitchen facilities in order to handle it. One such studio, shown here and on the following pages, was established in 1963 by Rudy Muller on the ground floor of a converted printing plant in New York City. In addition to a generously appointed kitchen *(above)*, it contains a carpentry shop for building sets and a shooting area of some 2,300 square feet. Like most studios it is amply equipped to take pictures of nonspecialized subjects. But a full 40 per cent of its billings come from photographing food.

◄ *In Rudy Muller's studio kitchen, a chef prepares a casserole of Flemish chicken that will be photographed as part of an assignment for American Home magazine. The magazine's food editor, Frances Crawford, busies herself over loaves of braided French bread. The chef, Jacques Jaffry, is employed by the client. Although Muller supplies the kitchen, the client does the cooking.*

Using an 8 x 10 view camera, Rudy Muller photographs, for American Home, a still life of assorted culinary delights, including the casserole being prepared on the opposite page. To give the picture a hearty, rustic look, the dishes are arranged on a plank table and an old barn door serves as one of the two background flats. The picture will be backlit. The light source is a large boxlike strobe unit at the rear, which is aimed through the space between the two flats. Cardboard reflectors in front of the table and above the camera fill in foreground shadows, and the two bulky floor batteries attached to cables at the right provide power for the strobe.

"Planning a still photograph is like putting together a movie," says Rudy Muller. "You have to put up a set, assemble the right props, and if you're using live models you have to find a cast." No casting was needed for the *American Home* assignment, which was simply to illustrate three traditional country recipes from Europe that would provide hot, one-dish meals for winter. Nonetheless, it took two days to set up the picture and photograph it.

The first step was a conference with the magazine's food editor and art director to plan the approach and decide on a set and props. Muller then built the set with the help of two assistants, while his stylist rummaged among the city's antique and gourmet-ware shops for appropriate plates, casserole dish-

es, pitchers and glassware. The next morning, a chef arrived from *American Home* to cook the food, which included a French *cassoulet* of beans and meat, Flemish-style chicken with cream and vegetables, and a stuffed cabbage. To make sure that the food would look fresh and appetizing during the entire shooting session, each dish was prepared in duplicate; when the first set of dishes became cold, it was replaced with the second set, which had been kept warm in the oven. As soon as the food was ready, it was arranged attractively on a table, the lighting was adjusted, and the shooting began. Muller photographed steadily for two hours, using both a 35mm reflex and an 8 x 10 view camera, and finally produced the picture on the opposite page.

Before shooting, Muller rearranges pieces of Flemish-style chicken in an earthenware casserole (above left) to make them more photogenic. He then photographs the assembled dishes with a 35mm camera (center), searching for unusual angles and depth-of-field effects. To create the effect of steam rising from the casseroles, an assistant gets ready to pump a liquefied titanium compound into the air above them. The chemical reacts with the air to produce a billowy, steamlike vapor.

RUDY MULLER: *One-Dish Meals*, 1970

The photograph picked to run in the magazine gives a hearty, down-home look to this array of sturdy provincial dishes, each one a meal in itself. The cassoulet is in the casserole at left, the chicken in the earthenware baking dish in the center, and the stuffed cabbage with tomato sauce on the plate at right. The rustic wine carafe, butter pot and lusterware pitcher were chosen to enhance the country-kitchen effect.

Producing Settings on Demand

One particularly specialized kind of studio photography is taking pictures of room settings. Furniture and fabric manufacturers, carpetmakers and makers of lighting fixtures all like to display their wares as though they had already been purchased and comfortably installed in the buyer's home. So for advertising photos they generally turn to studios that concentrate on designing and building homelike environments that attempt to give a lived-with look to a contemporary dining-room suite or an ensemble of matched bed sheets and window curtains.

A leading specialist in room-setting photography is Lionel Freedman, who in 1947 established his studio in New York City in a converted theater. There is something theatrical, in fact, about the whole Freedman establishment. He stages a photograph as though he were producing a play. The set is planned with the client in a conference room located on what was once the theater's balcony. It is designed by Freedman himself, who holds a degree in architecture from New York University. Sets are constructed and painted in a carpentry shop in the old backstage area and nailed together in the orchestra, where the photograph is shot. The final picture, processed in a darkroom in the balcony, is billed at orchestra prices —a minimum rate of $1,500 for a single-page advertisement designed to appear in a national magazine.

Working at a drafting table in his office (above left), Lionel Freedman designs a room setting for a client. The set will be built on the studio floor (left), and photographed with the view camera that is shown. The lighting console in the foreground works in much the same way as a stage electrician's light panel to produce an almost infinite variety of special effects.

In the orchestra of the converted theater that serves as Freedman's studio, an assistant assembles a room setting from a stockpile of flats and props. Freedman meanwhile roughs out another sketch in his office off the left side of the balcony. Freedman employs two assistants and occasionally hires professional carpenters and freelance stylists to help on difficult jobs.

This scaffoldlike object assembled from wooden struts in Lionel Freedman's studio is a 12-sided dome. It will provide the framework for a room setting designed to complement an arrangement of modern chairs, tables and bookcases. The client, S & H Green Stamps, will use the resulting photograph in a catalogue to show the various items—including furniture—that can be obtained for appropriate numbers of trading stamps.

LIONEL FREEDMAN: *Beach House*, 1970

The setting for the final photograph is a beach house laid out within the airy dome and filled with S & H furnishings. There are clean-lined tables, a chromium stand, a sectional bookcase and, hanging from a strut, an Op Art reproduction. The two models relax and ease back into chairs constructed like enormous plastic-covered bean bags. Two rear-projection screens provide the exterior background of beach and ocean.

Snow Scenes in July

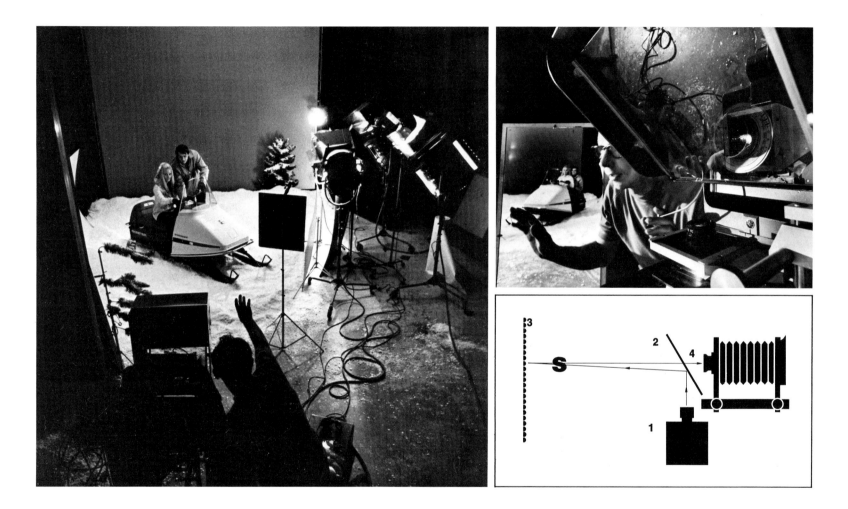

Versatility is the special strength of Pohlman Studios in Milwaukee, whose clients are mostly large manufacturing companies. Its facilities are so extensive that it can make almost any kind of photograph of any marketable product, from ketchup bottles to sailing yachts. One device allows products to be photographed in any imaginable setting without leaving the studio. Called a front projection system, it creates the same kind of panoramic vistas that early photographers produced with painted backdrops—but with far greater realism. Its components are a slide projector, a large screen with a special reflecting surface and a lightly silvered, see-through mirror that deflects light rays coming from one direction, but lets through rays coming from other directions *(diagram, right)*. By projecting the appropriate transparency, the photographer can shoot a sports car on a Daytona track, a surfer on a Hawaiian beach or a snowmobile *(opposite)*—all in Milwaukee in the middle of July.

Pohlman's front projection system creates the setting for a snowmobile ad. In the picture at left above, the photographer sets up his shot. The top picture shows the photographer by his camera, visible through the hooded mirror. The slide projector is below the camera lens, and the snowmobile is reflected in the mirror set behind the photographer's hand. The diagram illustrates the projection rig. The slide projector (1) beams a snow scene up at the lightly silvered see-through mirror (2), angled at exactly 45° in front of the camera. The mirror directs the image to the big screen (3). The snowmobile stands in front of the screen at S. The screen's surface has the ability to reflect light directly back toward its source, concentrating it so that the background seems very brightly lit. The intensified image returns through the mirror to the lens of the camera (4).

POHLMAN STUDIOS: *Snowmobile*, 1970

Though shot in the studio, the snowmobile and models seem to be outside on location. By carefully adjusting the lighting on the subject to match the brightness of the snowscape projected onto the background screen, the photographer has made the two blend together. The only props were plastic snow and the pine tree at right.

Room for Rent

The most unusual of all contemporary studios contains no cameras or darkrooms, not a single flood lamp or strobe unit. No photographers' names appear on its letterhead. Yet it provides two invaluable facilities for photographers —plentiful space and superb sets.

Classic Displays Incorporated started business in 1947 in New York City as an all-purpose set-design company. It planned and built displays for exhibition booths at trade fairs, showrooms for furniture stores, sets for fashion shows and window displays for department stores. But its talent for putting together distinguished sets on short notice quickly attracted photographers, who often need sets in a hurry but have neither space to house them nor facilities for constructing them. A photographer could order a set in the afternoon, and by next morning one would be built and ready for shooting.

As photography became an ever-greater part of CDI's business, and took over more and more of its floor space, CDI's founder Fred Rathe expanded into ampler quarters. In 1956 he purchased an entire six-story Victorian brick building *(opposite)* in New York City's Chelsea district. Like many other New York studios, the building is something of a mongrel. Built in 1903 as a stable for the draft horses that once pulled streetcars for the Fifth Avenue Coach Company, it has also been used as the headquarters of the Broadway stage-design firm of Nolan Brothers. Rathe converted it, installing carpentry shops, a metalworking shop, conference rooms, dressing rooms for models, and two studios measuring some 50 by 80 feet, which are rented out to photographers by the day. Because of its large size, and the multi-ton carrying capacity of its freight elevator, CDI is one of the few studios in the city equipped to handle large machinery, such as automobiles and trucks. Richard Avedon once used it to photograph an elephant, painted pink.

CDI is still a jack-of-all-trades in set design. "We build any kind of anything, for anybody," boasts the production manager Martin Freedgood. In addition to the usual trade exhibits and fashion shows, CDI has staged spectaculars such as the Hong Kong pavilion at the 1964-1965 New York World's Fair, for which it built three Chinese junks, the largest 40 feet long with a 32-foot mast. But photography seems to inspire its greatest feats of scenic legerdemain. It has churned up a rainstorm, built a miniature replica of Moscow's Red Square, and even created an Arctic ice floe, with styrofoam icebergs floating in a 60-foot-long ocean of real water. ☐

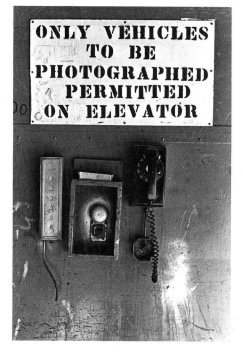

This sign is in CDI's freight elevator, once used to transport horses. Now it lifts automobiles up to the main studio area on the top floor of the fortresslike structure opposite, which was originally built as a horse barn.

Carpentry shops cover one entire floor of the CDI studio and spill over onto part of another. Here employees knock together flats, paint sets, prefabricate display booths and room settings for photographers and other commercial clients. The carpenters sometimes put in 80-hour weeks, working day and night to complete rush assignments. The workman in the picture on the opposite page, top left, puts finishing touches on a segment of a wooden archway for a trade fair; completed segments rest on his worktable. Another workman (opposite, bottom left) uses a band saw to cut a filigree in a board. To save time, sets are often fastened together with heavy-duty staple guns (opposite, top right) rather than hammer and nails. But more permanent props, such as the bookcase at bottom right, opposite, demand a cabinetmaker's painstaking skills.

In the main studio area on the top floor of the CDI building, a workman paints the cyclorama, a 70-foot-long plaster arc used as a permanent backdrop for photographs. The studio covers some 3,000 square feet and is 20 feet high. A tower above the roof allows camera heights of 30 feet.

CDI's heavy-duty freight elevator (above left) lifts a Ford Galaxie to the top-floor studio to be photographed for an ad. In the studio (above), a photographer lines up a shot of another car already parked in the cyclorama. Baffles at the right of the cyclorama and a ceiling of seamless paper direct light toward the subject. Since the sides of the cyclorama are curved, and the base slopes forward to meet the floor, avoiding a square joint, objects photographed within it appear to be suspended in infinite space.

A rain studio in CDI's ground-floor garage provides showers or hurricanes on order. The rain machine is simplicity itself—an overhead, perforated tin basin attached to a hose. Yet with appropriate backdrops, fans for simulating wind, and light reflectors (the umbrella at right in the picture above is for filling in shadows, not for keeping dry), photographers can blow up a thoroughly convincing rainstorm for overshoe and raincoat ads such as the shot at left.

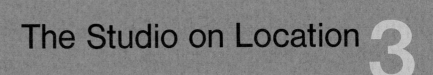

The Photographer's Team 80

On the Subject's Home Grounds 88

Working out of a Suitcase 92

Instant Setting in an Empty Flat 94

Irving Penn's Neutral Ground 98

*Members of the studio team at the major New ►
York firm of Horn/Griner gather on an office
stairway for a group portrait. At rear, under the
"G" of the firm's logotype, is general manager
Hal Siegman, wearing glasses and mustache.
Around him are people holding a variety of jobs,
from photographer's assistant and bookkeeper to
members of the television production unit.*

IRVING PENN: *Dahomey, Five Girls,* 1967

IRVING PENN: *Asaro Mudmen, New Guinea,* 1970

Focusing on Fashion 4

The High Art of Picturing Style 106

De Meyer: Mannered Chic 108
Steichen: Master of Lighting 110
Hoyningen-Huene: The Classic Ideal 112
Beaton: Borrowing from the Stage 114
Man Ray: Experimenting with Patterns 116
Munkacsi: The Drama of the Outdoors 118
Frissell: Playclothes in Faraway Places 120
Dahl-Wolfe: A Sense of Color and Setting 123
Horst: Highlighting the Sitter 124
Penn: Cool Elegance 127
Avedon: Emphasizing the Bizarre 128

Celebrating Today's World 130

Employing the Element of Shock 132
Glorifying the Object 134
Style for a Dehumanized Society 136
Sex in the Seventies 138
A Turn to Realism 140

EDWARD STEICHEN: *An early fashion photograph of a dress by designer Paul Poiret, Paris,* 1911

The High Art of Picturing Style

One of the paradoxes of studio photography is its most glamorous specialty: fashion. The pictures, at their best, are technically expert, esthetically valid and in some cases so beautiful that they are cherished among the finest examples of photographic art. Their appearance in print commands such great attention that fashion assignments attract the best photographers.

Yet fashion photography is as ephemeral as a woman's whim. Its subject matter is severely limited: it consists, amid whatever props, of a model wearing a stylish outfit. The photographer's problem is somehow to give freshness and variety to pictures that, as Edward Steichen *(pages 105, 110-111)* has said, "tell the same story year after year. All he has to present are photographs of the newest fashions." It is hardly a simple problem.

As for the purpose of fashion photography, it may seem simple—a selling job, to put it crassly—but in fact it is actually quite complex. It is the same multiple purpose that is served by the fashion magazines themselves: for one thing, to go out into the dream world of "beautiful people"—the modish and sophisticated, nice-smelling and certainly well-off—and to report back to less-favored people what these trend-setters are wearing, how they are eating, what they are reading, where they are congregating. The purpose goes deeper: to use this "in" world to influence the way ordinary people live, to trade them up from Miami Beach vacations to Montego Bay, from beef stew to beef Wellington—and in the process, to create an atmosphere that will induce readers to buy what is advertised in the magazines, and to dress, even by sew-it-yourself means, after the fashion of the fashion models.

The photographer has several people looking over his shoulder to remind him of this: the dress or accessory designer, the manufacturer, and—since all fashion photographs are meant for publication—a fashion editor and an art director. They help, but it is his imagination, more than proficiency, that is his trustiest weapon. Combined with his innate taste, it enables him to do his job, as defined by Cecil Beaton *(pages 114-115):* "The dressmaker provides the dress, but the photographer must make the woman in that dress appear in a manner that will give all other women a feeling of covetousness."

What often makes women covetous is the sight of another woman inhabiting that desirable world of well-heeled luxury. Some of the most successful photographers of the 1920s and 1930s were aided in creating such a world pictorially by their own real-life familiarity with it. There was Beaton, son of a British timber merchant, who went from the best schools (Harrow and Cambridge) into the top strata of London society, where he indulged twin tastes for party-going and dressing up: he once eschewed conventional dress to appear in a different fancy-costume disguise every day for 10 days. There was the pioneer Gayne de Meyer *(pages 108-109),* whose wife reportedly was the illegitimate daughter of Edward VII and who had a Venetian palace, a London town house and a home in the south of England, all rumored to be provided by his royal connection. De Meyer was a stoutish, cane-sporting exotic: he slept under a blanket of mink and protected his blue-dyed hair with a net while working in the studio. There was George Hoyningen-Huene *(pages 112-113);* he rarely used his title of baron and cultivated left-wing friends, but he also kept a picture of his father, a Baltic nobleman, in full regalia preceding the Czar in the 1896 coronation procession in Moscow. Huene had a fabled temperament: when he was working for *Vogue,* the magazine's art director Mehemed Fehmy Agha, acting on orders, took him to lunch one day and gently suggested that he "behave." Huene upset the table, food and all, right into Agha's lap, ran to the restaurant's telephone booth and called *Harper's Bazaar,* which hired him on the spot. (Agha, a colorful personality in his own right, was the Ukrainian-born son of a Turkish landowner and tobacco grower. A witty raconteur, he was credited with finally laying to rest certain fashion-photography clichés from the De Meyer days by deriding them in a 1939 memo to *Vogue* President Condé Nast: "To be alluring, a model must clutch her hips; to be glamorous, she must lean over backwards; to be dramatic, she must clutch a drape.")

The personal flamboyance of those older photographers has given way before the no-nonsense breed of studio men who produce the fashion shots of the 1970s *(pages 130-140).* The work of this new breed shows a wider variety of influences—social, esthetic and moral. If there is one constant that typifies their generation, it is something quite different from the earlier tendency to make the woman of fashion photographs a passive and overindulged daughter of privileged society. Today's practitioners are apt to try to illuminate some aspect of the inner life of the model, whom they see as a complex human being rather than a decorative clothes hanger. Many of them hope the picture will make a statement about the modern woman's psyche and her role in contemporary life—an ambition that perhaps reflects the anxiety of a world whose values are being challenged as never before.

The problems inherent in fashion photography—the narrowness of its subject matter, its make-believe milieu, its commercial aspect, the plethora of patrons whom it must please—have stimulated some of the world's most gifted photographers in the half century in which it has developed into a specialty. Beautiful clothes and models can provide inspiration, but the photographer must have the talent, skill and patience to work out a style so individualized that his work can be identified at a glance. The pictures on the pages that follow bear the photographers' signature as surely as if they had written their names on the negatives. In meeting their own exacting standards, they have also established fashion photography—whatever its humble origins as the appendage of an industry—as an art in its own right.

De Meyer: Mannered Chic

Prior to World War I the clothes shown in fashion magazines were most often sketched with pen and ink. But in 1913 Condé Nast, then the new publisher of *Vogue* magazine, asked a dilettante photographer whose work he liked to try his hand at photographing fashions. The man was Gayne de Meyer, a Parisian of German ancestry who called himself a baron although his claim to the title was dubious. De Meyer became the pioneer who founded the profession of fashion photography. His success was based on his familiarity with the fashionable world of his time and his ability to interpret it pictorially, and on the ethereal quality of his photographs—which effect he got by veiling his lens with silk gauze and using soft backlighting.

When he died in modest circumstances in Los Angeles in 1946, De Meyer's style had long been passé. It had been superseded by a series of newer trends in fashion photography set by a small group of talented men and women. Each presented a very personal image of the world of fashion and the handsome women who inhabit it —and in doing so molded fashion itself and influenced all studio photography.

This study of a woman in a gold lamé costume was made by De Meyer in Europe, a few years before he came to the United States. Although not strictly a fashion photograph, it was the kind of deliberately blurred image of a richly gowned, glamorous female that led Condé Nast to hire De Meyer to photograph fashion for Vogue.

DE MEYER: *Woman with Cup,* c. 1910

De Meyer almost invariably posed his models standing with one hand firmly on hip, a stance that presumably spelled chic to the baron. At top left the actress Jeanne Eagels in an evening gown and, below, a male model showing off the latest in morning coats both strike the classic De Meyer attitude. At lower left the model's outfit is overwhelmed by her surroundings; De Meyer was also an interior decorator who often created luxurious settings for his fashion shots. Some of Vogue's wealthier readers were so taken with these ornate and exotic backgrounds that they commissioned him to create salons for their town houses.

DE MEYER: *Jeanne Eagels*, 1921

DE MEYER: *Woman with Oriental Plant*, date unknown

DE MEYER: *Male Fashion*, date unknown

Steichen: Master of Lighting

Edward Steichen concluded that when a woman saw a picture of a dress she should get "a very good idea of how it was put together and what it looked like." His decision to take photographs that would make crystal clear the fabric, cut and details of a costume resulted in a forthright style that broke with his predecessors' fussy romanticism.

It also led Steichen to embark on a long and intensive experimentation with lighting. He had been taking fashion photographs as early as 1911, and yet by 1923, when he was doing fashion photography for *Vogue,* he had never made indoor pictures with artificial light. Confronted by the studio electrician's insistence that he use a dozen klieg arc lamps to photograph his first dress for *Vogue,* Steichen took a four-ply thickness of bed sheets and draped it over the entire battery to make the light from the arc lamps appear to be natural illumination (his action moved the electrician to observe, "That guy knows his stuff"). But Steichen soon realized that electric light would be invaluable in giving variety as well as clarity to fashion pictures and began adding lights one at a time until, by the end of his years with *Vogue,* there were, in his own words, "lights going all over the place."

In the photograph at right, one of a series Steichen made beginning in 1924, he used a celebrated model, Marion Morehouse (later wife of the poet e.e. cummings), but set her against a plain background and in a simple composition that focused attention on her dress. Even when he used an absurd prop like the horse on the opposite page, Steichen aimed so many lights at the models, the horse and the reflecting white-tile backdrop that the emphasis was still on the lines of the white fashions themselves.

EDWARD STEICHEN: *Marion Morehouse, 1927*

EDWARD STEICHEN: *White Fashions,* 1935

Hoyningen-Huene: The Classic Ideal

GEORGE HOYNINGEN-HUENE: *Housecoat by Chanel,* 1931

During more than two decades as a fashion photographer, George Hoyningen-Huene refined a style that combined a personal fascination with femininity and a reverence for the art of ancient Western civilization. The son of a Baltic baron and his American wife, Huene (rhymes with "learner") had received a classical esthetic education growing up in the pre-Revolutionary Russian court of Czar Nicholas II. It was a world, as he said in later life, where "men were men and women were women—modern people seem so androgynous to me." To capture the feminine mystique he recalled from his childhood, Huene worked patiently with his models, encouraging them until he had "made them conscious of their femininity . . . and they looked as if they were about to be kissed."

The quality that he strove to bring out in photography had been best portrayed, he felt, by the ancient Greek sculptors' idealizations of female serenity. In his own most characteristic pictures, there was a sense of statuesque monumentality, humanized by the model's air of sweet tranquillity. She seemed a flesh-and-blood Grecian deity—an irresistible image that women sought to make their own by wearing clothes like those that hung so gracefully on Huene's poised figures.

"Texture, line, simplicity—these were the things he liked, the classic truth," said Katharine Hepburn of her friend Huene when he died in 1968. Here he emphasized texture and line by covering the pillars flanking the model with sheet metal and bouncing front spotlights off them, thus dramatizing the shimmering satin-lamé material of the simply cut robe.

The plaster torso in the background of this picture of a clinging crepe gown is almost a Huene trademark. His follower Cecil Beaton (overleaf) noted that Huene's absorption in classic art led him "to bring a whole new collection of properties to his studio: women were posed against Corinthian columns, casts of Hellenic horses, heads of Greek gods."

GEORGE HOYNINGEN-HUENE: *Evening Gown*, 1934

Beaton: Borrowing from the Stage

CECIL BEATON: *Evening Gown*, 1934

The fashion photography of Cecil Beaton foretold the renown he was later to gain as a stage and screen designer (of sets and costumes for the play *Coco* and the movie *My Fair Lady,* among others). His photographs, executed mostly in the 1930s, are stage productions in microcosm, featuring sets designed by Beaton (who also frequently painted them) and lighting that mimicked the spotlights of the Broadway and Piccadilly shows of the period. But, despite the theatricality, Beaton pursued the realistic tradition: the clothes and the accessories were always as much stage center as the model.

Often the model was a well-known actress. Beaton was one of the first photographers to sense that stage and screen stars were desirable mannequins—their strong personalities enhanced the clothes they wore, and their well-publicized glamor aided in popularizing fashions.

A fast worker—he averaged 60 exposures during a two-hour sitting—Beaton was at the time somewhat self-consciously uninterested in technical procedure. He once said that he was "ashamed at being so inept at the technical side of the game," but he also rather enjoyed the amazed reaction of his listeners when he let it be known that he had taken his first pictures for *Vogue* with a hand-held, pocket-sized, folding Kodak No. 3A that was precariously set on a rickety old tripod.

Beaton staged the tableau at left by placing three models behind a backlighted, translucent screen of white muslin to produce the shadow silhouettes of a flower woman (left) and two beaux offering violets to a puppet-goddess of the haut monde arrayed in a costly formal gown.

CECIL BEATON: *Spring Fashion*, 1949

*A favorite Beaton device was to "embower"
his models in mixed real and artificial flowers.
Above, he used it to create a Vogue cover
by having the model put her head through
a hole in a canvas that he had decorated.*

*Beaton produced a series of "playlets"; this
one (right) starred the comedienne Ilka Chase as
a jilted girl. Hopefully the unhappy ending
would not deter women from buying the Henri
Bendel gown and Tiffany jewelry she was wearing.*

CECIL BEATON: *The Florist's Box*, 1937

Man Ray: Experimenting with Patterns

MAN RAY: *Gown by Schiaparelli, 1935*

Man Ray, a devotee of the iconoclastic artistic movement known as Dadaism, brought its ideas to the pages of high-style magazines. A fashion photographer from 1921 to the early 1940s, Man Ray was perfectly capable of executing relatively conventional pictures *(left)* of a suitably romantic nature. More often he used specialized darkroom techniques—many of them conceived by Man Ray himself—in creating photographs the like of which had never appeared on the fashion scene.

Man Ray would tilt his easel when enlarging a picture to create a startlingly elongated silhouette of model and costume or, using the technique known as solarization, expose a partly processed picture to reverse some tones, black for white and white for black. Man Ray's farthest-out innovation was something he called the "Rayograph"—a picture like the one opposite, made in the darkroom by placing various objects on a piece of printing paper and briefly exposing both to light. Such shadow pictures were not original with Man Ray, but the abstractions he created in them produced a surrealistic chic.

The Hindu-inspired dress at left was designed by Elsa Schiaparelli. For this picture, taken at the 1935 Paris showings, Ray avoided his intricate innovations. The picture was to be radioed to New York, a practice followed by Vogue and Harper's Bazaar. Man Ray realized that the infant art of radiophotography, with its observable scanning lines, would itself produce an unusual picture.

Man Ray made one of his celebrated Rayographs ▶ to convey an impression of the new fashions coming over the radio waves. This Rayograph, used in Bazaar, was produced by placing a cut-out elongated silhouette of a model and a piece of the loosely woven material of her gown atop a piece of printing paper. The material's honeycomb effect suggested a radiophoto's lines.

MAN RAY: *Fashion Rayograph*, 1934

Munkacsi: The Drama of the Outdoors

MARTIN MUNKACSI: *Beach Fashion*, 1936

When Martin Munkacsi arrived in the United States in 1934, he had been the highest-paid news photographer both in his native Hungary and later in Germany. Engaged at *Harper's Bazaar* by a new editor who gave him a free hand, though she knew he had not done fashion work, Munkacsi startled competitors with his first picture.

For a bathing-suit feature he took his model out of the studio to a windy Long Island beach, and insisted that she run toward him. Such action poses had never been used for fashion, and Munkacsi's pictures were tartly dismissed by *Vogue's* chief editor as "farm girls jumping over fences." Yet the image he created of the American woman swinging into splendid action out of doors became an enduring rival to the pampered creature who had adorned earlier fashion photography.

Her boldly striped beach coat billowing behind her, Munkacsi's model strides into the wind—a good illustration of his advice, published in Harper's Bazaar in 1935: "Never pose your subjects. Let them move about naturally. Don't let the girl stop to put her hair to rights."

A brave model perched on a parapet of a ▶ futuristic building at the 1939 New York World's Fair holds on to the wall with one hand as Munkacsi records his arresting view of a winter outfit (right). He once persuaded a reluctant model to sit on the back of a live camel by taunting her with the epithet "Supercoward!"

118

MARTIN MUNKACSI: *For the Winter Season*, 1939

Frissell: Playclothes in Faraway Places

Photographing fashion out of doors became a dominant trend during the late 1930s and into the 1940s as more and more women entered the active world outside the home. The sportswoman was a new female idol and to keep her free and easy, the fashion industry brought out bigger and better lines of sports- and playclothes. The outstanding photographer of outdoor wear was a young society woman named Toni Frissell, who preferred to shoot on location because she was "never mechanically minded" enough to feel at ease among the lights and equipment of the studio. But she had received good training on how to take pictures out of doors from her brother Varick, who had been a newsreel cameraman before his early death.

Besides her own talent, Miss Frissell brought two other advantages to the growing fad for sporty fashion photography: an ardent sportswoman herself (on an assignment, she once worked out with the United States Olympic ski team), she knew how to pose her athletic models convincingly, and how best to display the functional nature of their riding habits or tennis dresses.

Moreover, as a fully accredited Manhattan social registerite, she was able to take her models into exclusive watering places of the rich, such as Bailey's Beach in Newport or Cypress Point in California *(opposite)*. When *Vogue* or *Harper's Bazaar* subscribers examined a playdress photographed in such sacrosanct settings, their urge to acquire it was presumably strengthened.

TONI FRISSELL: *Bikini, 1946*

An alert Harper's Bazaar editor, spotting her first bikini on the French Riviera in 1946, sensed its imminent popularity and assigned Toni Frissell to picture it. Miss Frissell transported a model and a bikini to fashionable Montego Bay, Jamaica, and arranged the model on the pier at an hour when the sunlight would cast shadows long and dramatic enough to emphasize the contours of the girl's body. Result: the first picture of a bikini to be seen in a U.S. magazine.

Offering her face to the sun and the wind, a model in a characteristic Frissell pose shows off what was described as "the summer uniform of the land," a shirtwaist dress. The setting is a beach resort at Del Monte, California, where the sports-loving rich disported themselves amid surrealistic cypress trees and barking seals.

TONI FRISSELL: *Shirtwaist*, 1938

Mrs. Wolfe used Kodachrome film in an 8 x 10 view camera to record the delicate hues of this photograph. To set off the old-fashioned charm of the lace-trimmed nightgown that is th focal point of the picture, she employed the Victorian setting of her own New Jersey bedroc A decorator like Gayne de Meyer (pages 108-1 Mrs. Wolfe followed the studio-photographer's tradition, not only choosing film and arranging lighting, but selecting all the props for her set.

LOUISE DAHL-WOLFE: *My Bedroom*, 1942

Dahl-Wolfe: A Sense of Color and Setting

LOUISE DAHL-WOLFE: *Sun Fashion*, 1952

Louise Dahl-Wolfe was a painter and decorator turned photographer, with an intense interest in color that led her to pioneer its use in fashion pictures. In the 1930s, when she started taking fashion pictures, black-and-white was thought preferable for this medium because even slight deviations from the true colors of the fashions could cause the photograph to be rejected. Though Kodachrome, the first modern color film, became available after 1935, it could not always be counted on to produce true colors, in or out of doors. Mrs. Wolfe worked under strong klieg lights in the studio, using huge one-shot cameras *(page 58)*. She trained herself with diligence, absorbing all she could from camera technicians and engravers, and by the time she retired from the field in 1962, she had contributed such "firsts" as the atmospheric photograph on the opposite page. It is perhaps the earliest color fashion photograph to use interior natural light, a difficult achievement during this period of still-erratic film.

After World War II, Mrs. Wolfe helped introduce another innovation by taking her models to little-known spots almost anywhere on earth and photographing them against such exotic settings as the ruins of ancient civilizations *(left)*. The effect was to add another dimension to the image of the outdoor girl Munkacsi and Frissell had glorified, by making her a citizen of the world.

Photographer and model traveled to the Maya ruins in Mexico's Yucatán peninsula to make this picture of smartly matched shorts and top posed against a stone where human sacrifices had been offered to propitiate the gods.

Celebrating Today's World

The fashion photographers of the 1970s often borrow techniques from various styles of modern art: Impressionism, Symbolism, Surrealism, even Cubism *(pages 131-135)*. Like the painters who first developed these techniques, the photographers who adapted them to fashion work in the 1960s became embroiled in controversy. Late in 1965, Norman Norell, a top United States designer, expressed the annoyance of his fellow couturiers: "Fashion photographers have really gotten out of hand. They distort a suit or dress beyond recognition." His well-known colleague James Galanos agreed: "The important point of fashion is too often lost because the photographer gets involved in the model or the scene he is shooting —everything but the dress."

Fortunately for the photographers, the fashion editors tended to side with them. The fashion director of *Harper's Bazaar* thought the complaints "come from designers who are older and not with it." *Vogue's* editorial director said, "Though some of them undoubtedly prefer the . . . conventional photograph, most designers are happy to be part of an avant-garde development."

The acceptance of some distortion in fashion photographs enabled the photographers to give their work a really contemporary look. And that, according to Bert Stern, is where it's all at. "The photographer has to respond to today," he says. "If he doesn't, he's getting himself ready to be obsolete." For Stern this response can take the form of a pictorial comment on technology and its effects on society *(pages 136-137)*. For Hiro, borrowing a leaf from the book of his mentor Richard Avedon *(page 128)*, it may involve using "contemporary models for the contemporary focus": discovering, for example, the striking women to be found in such previously unfashionable societies as Puerto Ricans in the East or *chicanos* in the West. Hiro is also intrigued by the space age: his contract with *Harper's Bazaar* stipulates that he will be the first fashion photographer the magazine sends to the moon.

The fashion photographer of the '70s reflects trends in contemporary life in a way that would sadly perplex his professional ancestor, Gayne de Meyer. He photographs fashion accessories so that they seem to loom larger than life *(pages 134-135)* because for many hell-bent consumers such goods really do have grotesquely immense importance. He makes his pictures more explicitly sexy *(pages 138-139)* because the climate of today's world is sexually liberated. He has created an image of an existence *(page 140)* that is concerned more with a down-to-earth life style and the clothes that are appropriate to it, than with the elusive fantasies of leisured elegance for the few.

During their Cubist phases Pablo Picasso and ► Georges Braque, following Cubism's practice of breaking up a subject into many facets, painted portraits that showed their subjects from several viewpoints. Mel Sokolsky used the same idea when he was commissioned to make a photograph (opposite) illustrating eye and lip make-up. The usual method of creating multiple-image pictures is to place one negative on top of another and print them on the same sheet. The problem is that the photographer does not actually see the images in combination until the print is developed. Sokolsky wanted to exert control over his design from the beginning, so he placed an earlier-made slide showing the model's profile in a projector and threw its image on her features as she sat facing him. He used the projector's zoom lens to adjust image size until he got exactly the effect he wanted and then snapped the shutter on his 35mm Canonflex. He floodlit the wall behind the model with very bright light to wash out that portion of the projected profile-image that otherwise would have spilled over onto the left-hand background. His two-faced image is a useful fashion shot because it offers a double display of the effect of the make-up; but Sokolsky says that, like the Cubist painters and others before them, he was also using the double image to comment on the dual nature of every woman's inner self.

ART KANE: *New York Woman,* 1970

Glorifying the Object

SILANO: *Handbag, 1967*

The tendency of an affluent society to glorify its goods is nicely exemplified in the photographs of William Silano. He likes to take pictures of inanimate objects that present them as substantial, even monumental, images. Moving in close to his subject and shooting from an angle slightly below it, he gives fashion accessories gigantic proportions that vastly increase their impressiveness. He also favors surrealistic color and lighting effects: he believes that by creating a mystery and "tension" between the object and its surroundings, he endows it with a pictorial life of its own. At his most successful, Silano transforms commercial products into colossal images that all but command materialists to worship them.

Silano took the photograph of a handbag at left from a distance of two or three feet, standing on the roof of his New York City studio. He perched the bag on a ledge covered with brown seamless paper and placed a small mirror so that it reflected the light from the noonday sun (visible just behind the bag, on the left) onto the front of the bag. Angle and lighting were planned to make the bag seem to be a gargantuan object looming on the horizon against the light of dawn.

The ski boot opposite was photographed on the ▶ shore of Long Island Sound. It was a summer afternoon, so Silano simulated ice on the ground by melting a quarter-inch-thick sheet of clear plastic, on which he set the boot. To give the landscape its unnatural yet provocative colors, Silano shot his picture on infrared film.

SILANO: *Ski Boot,* 1967

Style for a Dehumanized Society

ALBERTO RIZZO: *Belts, 1970*

Bert Stern took the picture opposite at the Paris showing of André Courrèges's 1969 collection. Stern likes the designer's tendency to bare the body because he believes that the physical presence of the human being should be stressed in the face of the menace of the machine. Here he wanted to make the models in their microdresses appear to be pitting their flesh—however pitiably—against the threatening forces in today's technological environment. So he posed them marching in lock step like so many robots.

On the other hand, when Alberto Rizzo was commissioned to photograph fashions in belts, he created deliberately depersonalized images *(left)*. To dehumanize his models he dressed them in the anonymity of leotards, posed them against an aseptic white background and aimed his camera to crop any individualizing features, such as heads, legs or arms.

To elongate the models' torsos (left), Alberto Rizzo shot his picture with an anamorphic lens. Such lenses compress one dimension of an image but leave the other dimension unchanged. Here he adjusted the lens to squeeze the horizontal image into snakelike lengthiness.

Stern used Courrèges's own showroom ▶ mannequins instead of photographic models in the picture opposite because they knew how to move, and motion was important to the concept of his picture. Since their faces were not as conventionally photogenic as those of photographic models, he partially obscured their features with Courrèges-designed Dynel wigs.

BERT STERN: *Metal Dresses*, 1969

Sex in the Seventies

The picture at right appeared in the August 15, 1963, issue of *Vogue.* The model's bare bosom was implied rather than flaunted. Nevertheless, the photograph marked the advent of the sexual revolution of the '60s, a phenomenon that caused a new freedom in fashion and its photography. Thereafter bras dropped, as *Vogue* put it, "like autumn leaves," and pictures of the topless monokini replaced the bikini in the pages of the magazine, accompanied by advice to readers on how to be "seen proudly uncovered." Ultimately, *Vogue* got around to a stylish version of a *Playboy* magazine staple: a centerfold, double-truck nude girl; she was photographed by Irving Penn.

Men got into the act in 1968, when the French fashion journal *Elle* published a head-on photograph of a male nude, in an ad for underwear. The next step was to bring men and women together in fashion pictures, with the male model presented not as the admiring background figure of the past but in a more candidly sexual role. By the start of the '70s, men and women were exhibiting togetherness in high-fashion photographs, clothed to be sure, but often intertwined *(opposite).*

To photograph an example of the heavy, textured hosiery that was then the latest thing (right), Art Kane took advantage of the new sexual freedom to create a scene suggesting an elegant, European-type brothel, and presented his model as an infinitely more accessible type than the old-style untouchable mannequin. And the German photographer H. P. Mühlemann, assigned to illustrate the desirable flexibility of synthetic-fiber knitwear, draped his models in a tenderly intimate pose (opposite) of slightly understated eroticism.

ART KANE: *Girl in Blue Stockings,* 1963

H. P. MÜHLEMANN: *Medico's Boutique Fashions*. 1970

A Turn to Realism

The kind of glamor synthesized by others in the field of fashion photography is gone from the picture at right by Alen MacWeeney. So is the assumption that in fashion the world is always happy and bright: it is a gray day and rain beats against the windowpane. MacWeeney feels that to survive as an art form, fashion photography will reach closer to reality in its reportage: a record of what real-life men and women will wear while pursuing their daily routines in their ordinary surroundings. The photographer will get his best effects by shooting on location, choosing sites that are accessible or familiar to the public to give his backgrounds the force of authenticity. He will use non-professional models, people who are fat, thin, young, old, sleek or dowdy —anything, as long as they are photographically interesting. His picture may be tinged with social comment, but never tainted with the appeal to snobbish instincts that long characterized much fashion photography. Thus MacWeeney's fashionable world of the 1970s is a relaxed and realistic place where everyone is free to do his own thing. □

Seated on a window ledge at the Chelsea, a venerable Manhattan hotel frequented by artists and writers, a leggy girl in a simply cut minidress kibitzes, ignored by her card-playing boyfriends. She is a far cry from the pampered woman whose regally self-assured presence, photographed against extravagant backgrounds, symbolized the woman of fashion in the past.

ALEN MacWEENEY: *Winter Day,* 1969

Inside the Modern View Camera 144

The View Camera's Limitations 146
The Four Camera Movements: 1 | Rise and Fall 148
The Four Camera Movements: 2 | Shift 150
The Four Camera Movements: 3 | Tilt 152
The Four Camera Movements: 4 | Swing 154
Combining Fall, Swing and Tilt to Make a Still Life 156
Obtaining Infinite Depth of Field 158
Dealing with Distortion 159
Removing the Unwanted from a Picture 160
Selecting a Point of Emphasis 162
Changing the Look of a Skyscraper 164
Overlapping for a Wider Wide-Angle 166
The Camera as Magnifier 168
Creating the Illusion of Motion 170

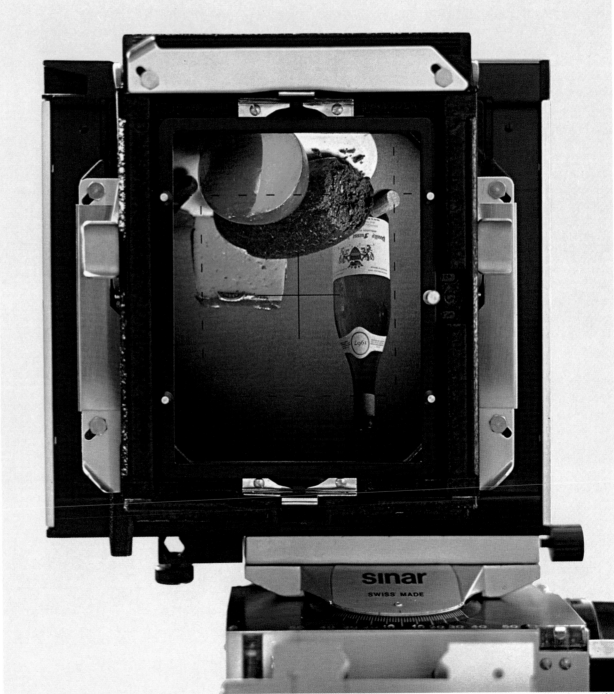

KEN KAY: *Still Life as Seen on the Ground-Glass Screen of a View Camera*, 1970

Inside the Modern View Camera

One of the things that cost money in a high-quality camera is precision. Consider, for example, the relation of film and lens: to ensure sharp overall focus, they must be lined up absolutely parallel, one squarely behind the other. If they are not—if the lens is the least bit out of line or if the film is not held exactly straight behind the lens—the picture will be marred by soft or blurry spots that no amount of careful focusing can possibly eliminate.

What is the purpose, then, of paying a good deal of money (from $100 to $1,500 without lens) for a view camera whose film and lens can be deliberately "unaligned"? Because in trained hands this can make it possible to take pictures that a rigid camera, no matter how expensive, simply cannot produce. An obvious example is trying to photograph a tall building from across the street. Tip the camera up to include the top, and the entire building seems to fall over backward in the finished photograph. If it were possible to lower the film in the back of the camera so that it recorded a different part of the image projected by the lens, then considerably more of the building could be included within the frame of the picture.

This is only one of the adjustments that can be made by the view camera, whose back (film) and front (lens) can be independently twisted and moved in a number of directions: up, down or sideways, tilted forward or back, swiveled to either side. Each of these movements has a different effect on the negative. If properly understood, they can be used to impart an extraordinary amount of discipline and control to photography. They can eliminate or increase distortion; they can straighten up walls, pull things into or out of focus, change perspective. How these movements are accomplished mechanically in a camera is shown in the diagram opposite. What they do photographically is explained on the next 26 pages.

In describing these movements the directions given relate, for consistency and clarity, not to the inverted image shown on the view camera's ground-glass viewing screen, but to the photograph that is actually taken.

Two basic movements that can be made with the front and back of the view camera are loosely known to photographers as swings and tilts. Swings are movements around the *vertical* axis of either lens or film—i.e., when either is twisted to the left or right. Tilts are movements around the *horizontal* axis of lens or film—i.e., when either is tipped forward or backward.

In addition to these two movements, many view cameras provide two others. One is sideways movement of lens or film to either left or right; this is known as shift. The other is raising or lowering of lens or film; this is known as rise or fall. These four movements can be used separately or in combination, according to the practical or esthetic need of the photographer. A camera that provides all of them is the most versatile instrument known to photography.

parts

A | lens
B | aperture scale
C | shutter-speed scale
D | lens board
E | lens-board-adjustment thumbscrew
F | front standard
G | front-standard-adjustment thumbscrew
H | shutter-release cable
J | bellows
K | tripod mount
L | ground glass
M | back-adjustment thumbscrew
N | back
O | back standard
P | back-standard-adjustment thumbscrew
Q | dark slide
R | film holder
S | film sheet

movements

1 | back-rise
2 | back-fall
3 | front-rise
4 | front-fall
5 | back-shift left
6 | back-shift right
7 | front-shift left
8 | front-shift right
9 | back-tilt backward
10 | back-tilt forward
11 | front-tilt backward
12 | front-tilt forward
13 | back-swing left
14 | back-swing right
15 | front-swing left
16 | front-swing right
17 | front focusing
18 | back focusing

This simplified cutaway of a view camera makes ▶ clear its basic relationship to all cameras: it is a box with a lens at one end and a sheet of film at the other. Unlike other cameras, however, the box is not rigid. The front face, to which the lens is fastened, can be moved independently—up or down, tilted forward or back—by loosening a pair of thumbscrews (E). A second pair of thumbscrews (M) permits similar movements of the back. Two other thumbscrews (G and P) permit front or back to be shifted, swung or focused. In addition, different-sized film can be used by substituting film holders and camera-backs that are designed for those sizes. Furthermore, the front end of the camera will accept different lenses, and extra bellows can be inserted between front and back (page 168) to accommodate their different focal lengths and to provide extreme extensions for close-up work. Finally, if the focal length of the lens is so short that the regular bellows cannot be squeezed tight enough, it can be removed, and a special bag bellows substituted (page 158).

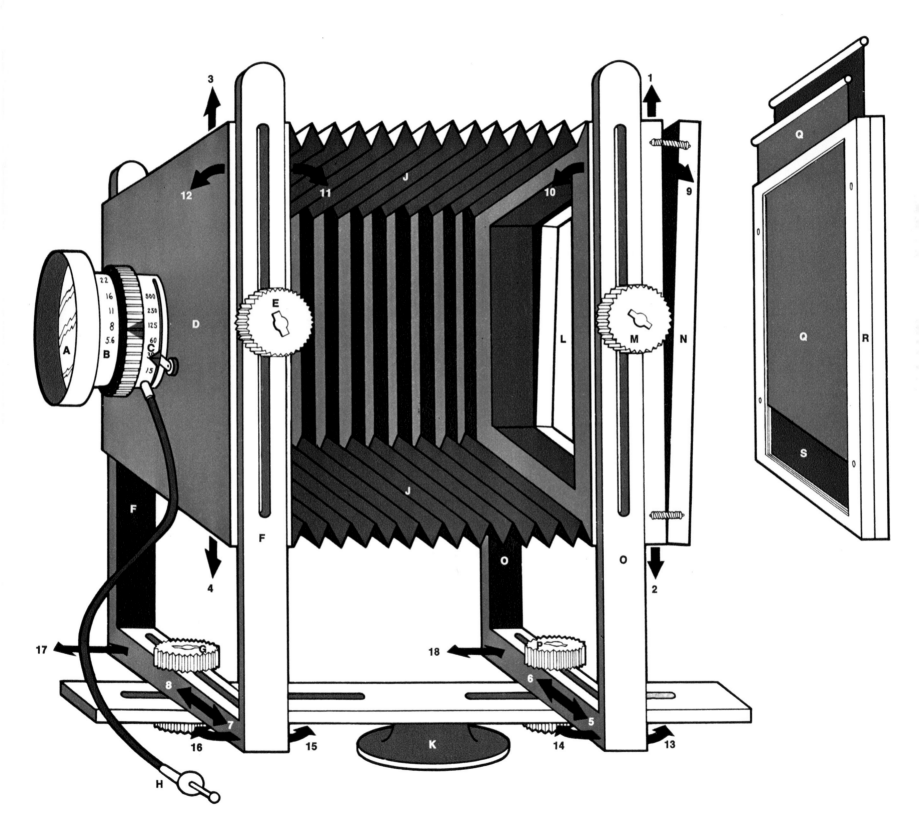

Combining Fall, Swing and Tilt to Make a Still Life

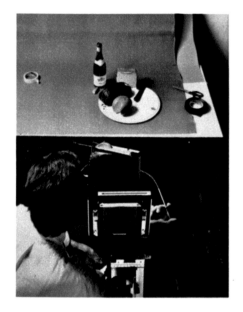

Here is the setup of Ken Kay's still life just before the final shot was made. Note the extreme right-swing of the front of the camera to get sharp focus on the bottle, the bread and the round cheese.

A still life consisting of a bottle, bread and a couple of cheeses was set up in his studio by photographer Ken Kay for a shot angled slightly downward at the arrangement. With his view camera in the right position, and with all settings at zero, Kay found several things wrong with the picture when he studied it on the ground glass of his camera. But by cranking adjustments into the camera one at a time, he was able to get an approximation of the picture he wanted. That shot *(fourth picture at right)* was, however, too far out of focus in some spots to satisfy him. Since he was working in a studio with control over his light, this was no problem. Simply by stopping his lens way down *(last picture)*, Kay was able to produce the degree of sharpness he was after.

As a starter, Kay placed his camera at the desired angle with all controls set at zero. Here he is interested only in the relationship of objects: how much of the label is visible over the top of the bread, how the cut in the cheese looks, whether the cork is located properly. The setup is off center on the film, but that is of no concern as yet.

Kay's first adjustment is to bring the still life into proper position on the film. He does this with a simple fall of the camera-back. Although he plans ultimately to have the cheese in the foreground touch the bottom edge of the picture, he does not move it quite that far down at this stage because he will enlarge it with his next adjustment.

The next movement straightens up the bottle, which was leaning because of camera angle. Kay does it by back-tilt of the camera-back, using the same principle that straightened the lines on the reference cube (page 152). Back-tilt also enlarges the foreground cheese and positions it properly. But this puts some things badly out of focus.

Now Kay addresses himself to focus. Having decided that he wants the sharpest emphasis to be on the left edges of bottle, bread and foreground cheese, he swings his camera-front to the right to bring the focal plane closer to that line. Then he stops down his lens to f/22 and takes a picture that satisfies him (above right).

Obtaining Infinite Depth of Field

One of the most common frustrations experienced by the beginning photographer comes when he tries to photograph something like a field of daisies. If he is using a camera without swings or tilts, he is in trouble. To picture the daisies properly, he has to shoot down at an angle. Obviously, the most dramatic and interesting daisies will be those closest to the camera. But if he focuses on these, the background daisies will get hopelessly blurred—and vice versa. A compromise focus—one aimed at the middle of the daisy patch —might be all right if he stopped his lens way down to increase his depth of field. But this would require a long exposure, and since daisies tend to move in the breeze during long exposures, this solution may not work.

The view camera can get around this problem. It permits sharp focus from here to infinity at maximum apertures —if a principle discovered in the 19th Century is followed. This is the fine-sounding Scheimpflug Principle, which was named after its discoverer, an otherwise obscure Austrian surveyor.

Scheimpflug hit on the fact that if the plane of the film, the plane of the lens and the plane of the subject all meet on a common line, a picture of the subject will be sharp from near edge to far. This is demonstrated by the two setups at right. In the first a wide-angle lens was used in a view camera to shoot a carpet. No tilts or swings were made. As a result, the planes of lens and film are parallel. They do not converge, and the resulting picture is not sharp overall. But by tilting the lens forward, the planes can be made to converge—and by careful focusing, a picture of dramatic overall sharpness is possible.

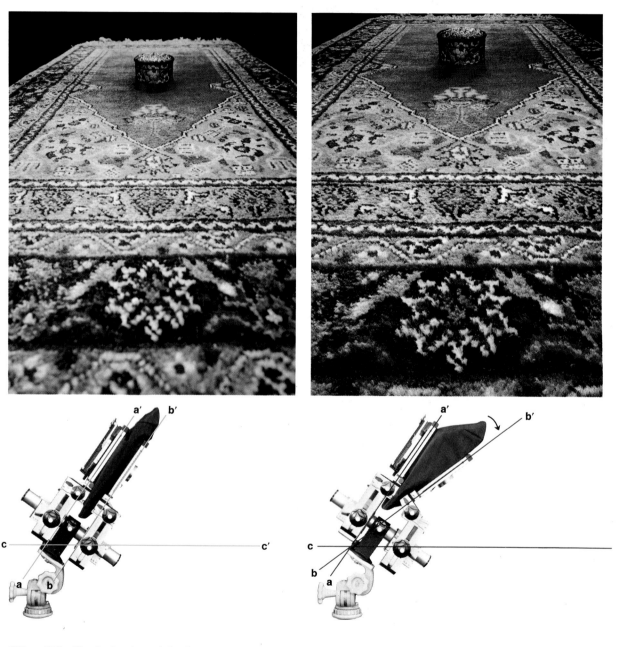

With no tilt in either back or front of the view camera, the plane of the film (line aa') cannot converge with the plane of the lens (line bb'). Therefore, they cannot meet the plane of the image (line cc') at the same point, as the diagram shows. Result, a picture that is partly out of focus.

By tilting the lens forward, its plane is changed, and now lines aa', bb' and cc' all converge, to produce a picture that is sharp overall. But the focal length of the lens was so short (65mm) that a loose bag bellows had to be substituted for the regular accordion-type bellows.

Dealing with Distortion

Every attempt to project a three-dimensional object onto a two-dimensional surface results in a distortion of one kind or another. Yet cleaning up distortion in one part of a photograph will usually induce a different kind of distortion in another. The book and orange in the two still lifes at right are examples of this. In the first picture, shot from above at a 40° angle with all camera adjustments at zero, the book shows two kinds of distortion. Since its bottom is farther away from the camera than the top, the bottom looks smaller. Also the book seems to be leaning slightly to the left. These effects would have been less pronounced if the camera had been farther away from the book —on the principle that the more distant an object is from a lens, the smaller will be the proportionate differences in distance from the lens to the center of the object and from the lens to the edge of the object. It is these differences that cause distortions in scale.

Can they be corrected? They can with a view camera, using a combination of tilts, swings and falls. Back-tilt of the camera-back straightens up the book's left edge. A left-swing of the camera-back squares up the face of the book. Fall of the back lowers the image—a necessity, since these tilts have enlarged the image somewhat.

A less distorted picture? That depends. The book is certainly squared up nicely, as if it were being looked at head on, but the spine is still visible. How can that be? Furthermore, the round orange of the first picture has now become somewhat melon-shaped. Moral: all pictures contain distortions; the photographer will have to manipulate them to suit his own taste.

With camera settings at zero, a downward view of a book makes the upper part seem larger than the lower part—just as the top-front edge of the cube on page 152 was larger than the bottom edge. This also makes the book appear to be tipping to the left. The orange, on the other hand, a sphere seen straight on in the center of the picture, exhibits no noticeable distortion.

The book is straightened up by back-tilt and left-swing of the back, but the orange is forced out of shape. These back movements also have had a bad effect on focus; it has been necessary to back-tilt the lens and swing it to the left to bring its plane into better line with the book's face.

Removing the Unwanted from a Picture

When the photograph immediately at right is studied, two awkward things become apparent about it. Both stem from the photographer's effort to get a formal, squared-up front view of a handsome Louis XV fireplace with its mirror, flanking pilasters, mantel clock and candlesticks at the Metropolitan Museum of Art in New York.

The obvious way to get such a photograph is to place the camera squarely in front of the mirror. Unfortunately a large and distracting chandelier gets in the way, blocking the top of the mirror. Worse, a reflection of the photographer and the camera can be seen. Getting around these problems with an ordinary camera requires that the picture be taken from an angle—which produces a routine shot *(second picture)* that loses the desired frontal effect. The view camera, however, can get rid of the unwanted elements and still keep the frontal effect—by using shift.

As the earlier demonstrations with the cube made clear, a shift of the camera-back to the right will move the image on the film to the right. Shift of the camera-front to the left also will move the image to the right. A combination of the two will move the right-hand portion of the image off the film and replace it with another image that could not be captured (from that position) by an ordinary camera at all.

Back to the mirror: aiming the camera straight at the wall at a point to the right of the mirror, the photographer then shifts both front and back of the camera. The planes of the camera-back, the wall and the mirror remain parallel—thus achieving the desired frontal effect with neither photographer nor camera in the picture.

A head-on shot that guarantees a squared-up picture of the fireplace and its mirror is made impossible by the chandelier hanging in the way, and also by the reflection of the photographer, who can be clearly seen in the mirror.

Moving to one side gets rid of the chandelier and the reflection, but this introduces perspective distortion into the photograph, and the squared-up head-on effect that the photographer was anxious to achieve is lost entirely.

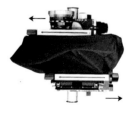

Aiming the camera directly at the wall a little to the right of the mirror squares up everything again. Then a right-shift of the camera-back and a left-shift of the camera-front pulls the image of the mirror back into the middle of the film.

Selecting a Point of Emphasis

Often a photographer wants to emphasize only one or two things in a picture by making them sharp and letting the rest of his composition go out of focus. This is easy enough if the singled-out objects are all the same distance from the lens; he need only focus on them, open his aperture wide, and the depth of field will be so narrow that the rest of the picture will become blurred.

But what if the objects are not the same distance from the lens? Only the view camera can handle this problem. If the reader has taken in the lessons given on pages 152-155, he will know that the solution is to swing the camera lens so that its focal plane is in line with the plane of the objects he wishes to emphasize. The two pictures opposite make this point.

The aim of the photographer was to focus sharply on a pile of beans spilling diagonally across a picture, and to let some of the surrounding jars go out of focus, keeping emphasis on the spilled beans. Since some of the beans are much nearer the lens than others, a rigid camera would have to be stopped way down in order to keep all the beans sharp. But this would bring the jars into focus too, as the top picture shows. By swinging the view camera lens and opening it wide, the photographer can create a narrow depth of field that follows the beans through the picture and leaves everything else blurred.

With camera-back and -front in zero position, a close-up shot of some spilled beans requires that the lens be stopped down to get both the foreground beans and those in the jar perfectly sharp. This also brings the other jars into focus.

A simple swing of the lens to the right brings its focal plane parallel to the receding pile of beans—all the way from the near-right foreground, back through the tipped-over jar. Now the photographer can focus on the beans and open up his lens to its maximum of f/5.6, which throws the other jars completely out of focus.

Creating the Illusion of Motion

A sense of movement can be imparted to a stationary object with a stationary camera—if that camera has rises and shifts. All that is required is a series of exposures on the same sheet of film, introducing a little more fall and shift with each exposure, to move the image on the film. In the picture at right, five exposures were made of a glass bird against a dark background, the back of the camera being increasingly lowered and shifted left each time. This photograph, like all the others in this chapter including the eight pages of cube demonstrations, was made by the New York photographer Ken Kay. ☐

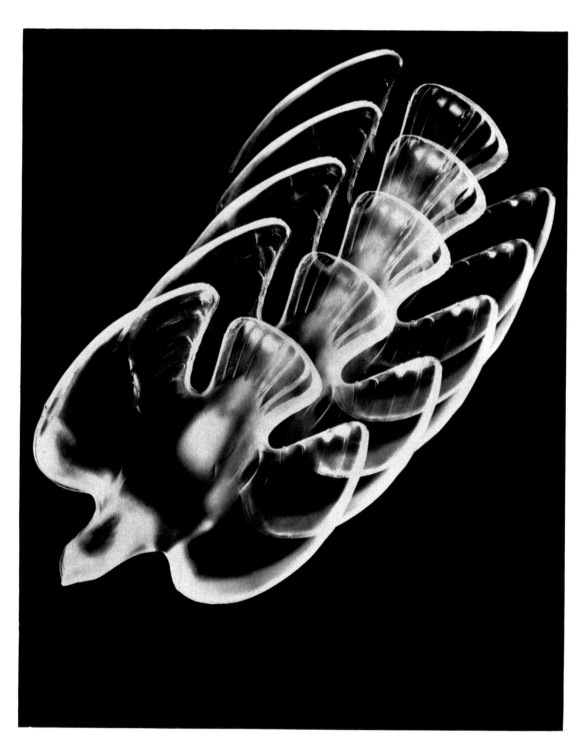

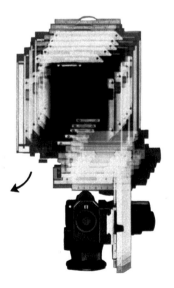

Falls and shifts, added in carefully graduated amounts for five successive exposures, produce a multiple-image shot of a glass bird that seems to swoop in a curve down through the picture. The only other help Kay gave the photograph was to dodge the bird's head to subdue its brightness. He did this with every exposure except the last.

HENRY WANTLAND: *Photo Studio in Stillwater, Oklahoma*, c. 1895

A Room of Your Own

There comes a time in the life of every amateur photographer when the thought begins nagging him that perhaps he might set up his own studio. This will probably stem from a desire to work under more controlled conditions and with larger cameras than are convenient for his outside work. Still-life experiments with varying light effects, like those shown on pages 202-211, may attract him. He may be ambitious to try serious portrait work. Or he may be stimulated by the opportunities for image control that the tilts and swings of the view camera provide *(Chapter 5).*

Whatever his motivation, a day will arrive when he will catch himself looking at his basement, his back hall or his garage in a new way, and asking himself some important questions: Just what is needed to set up a studio? How much space? What about plumbing and electric circuits? Must everything be set up all at once? Or can a small, inexpensive beginning be useful?

These are among the most elusive questions in photography because the answers depend entirely on what the photographer intends to do. A studio is really nothing more than a convenience. Some of the greatest pictures ever taken were made in studios that were ludicrously primitive—not because that was the way the photographer liked it, but because that was all he had for working space, and he was able to make do with it. Apartment bathrooms, even closets to which water must be lugged in pails, have made workable—if awkward—darkrooms. The one minimum requirement is enough space to use the camera and lights effectively. Other things can be improvised, but if a man's fancy runs to full-length portraits, he cannot operate properly in an eight-foot-square bedroom, even though such space would be adequate for tabletop still-life work.

So, in terms of the pictures that are to be made, consider space first. Additional space will probably be needed for developing and printing, as well as storage for equipment and supplies. Obviously, these functions are best handled when they are located together, but they do not have to be. It is possible to do all the photography in the garage and all the processing in the basement—and get exercise walking between the two.

The space problem is often the simplest to solve. Good organization and ingenious photographic solutions permit making quite ambitious pictures in places that, at first glance, might seem totally inadequate for the purpose. There is no better illustration of this last point than the studio of Al Freni, a successful professional who conducts an active business from minuscule quarters in a midtown New York skyscraper. Although the bulk of Freni's work is close-ups for advertisers, he can also handle surprisingly large subjects, like the model with bicycle shown on page 181. Since few amateurs —and not many professionals, either—will want to attempt anything much larger than Freni's bicycle shot, the dimensions of his studio can be taken as adequate for most uses—provided the space is used as intelligently and economically as Freni uses his. The layout and equipment that get so much from so little room are worth careful study.

The space Freni occupies measures 9 by 30 feet, with an 8½-foot ceiling. With a small darkroom tucked in the back, he is left with a 22-foot-long area for taking pictures. However, not all of that is usable photographic space. There must be room at one end for seamless paper rolls—the "no-seam" used for backgrounds—to hang from the ceiling behind his subject. The subject itself often will have to be moved out into the room, several feet in front of his background, if it is to be backlit. Also, the light stands must go somewhere, which cuts down on the usable width of the room.

One way that Freni has managed to work so well in such a small space is that he has gradually accumulated a good deal of specialized photographic equipment, which increases his flexibility. What another photographer could accomplish in one way in a larger studio, Freni can manage differently in his with different props, a different camera or a special lens. This is not to say that the prospective studio-builder should make up a shopping list from what Freni uses and head for his nearest photo supplier—the bill would run to several thousand dollars. Freni himself started with two cameras, a couple of tripods, some seamless paper rolls, a table and a few lights, adding equipment as he needed it and could afford it. The reader should follow the same rule: buy nothing unless there is a specific use for it; otherwise the precious working space will shrink away little by little, and the photographer will eventually discover that he no longer has a studio but, instead, a storage room. This is a hard tendency to resist, but it should be resisted at all costs.

Freni has also saved space by putting pegboards and shelves on his walls, cupboards under all flat working surfaces. He is extremely neat. Everything has its place, and it is all carefully put away after each shooting session. He gains some additional compactness in his darkroom because it is set up to process only black-and-white film. Although he shoots a great amount of color, he finds it tricky and time-consuming to process himself, so he sends it to an outside firm.

Skimpiness in fundamental equipment, however, is false economy. An ample electric supply is, of course, a must, since some studio lights drain a good deal of power. If a 220-volt line is installed, it can be wired to supply a large number of 115-volt outlets, so that the load can be evenly distributed among them without overtaxing any one. Hot and cold running water should be available for the darkroom. In most homes the best place to find easy access to utilities—along with working space and simplicity of light-proofing—is in a basement laundry, which may even have a pair of old laundry sinks already in place, almost begging to be used to process film.

1 | entrance door
2 | telephone and telephone
   answering device
3 | pegboard with tools
4 | storage shelves
5 | light box for viewing transparencies

6 | cabinet desk
7 | electronic-flash heads
   and reflectors
8 | electronic-flash power packs

9 | electronic-flash
   unit with umbrella
10 | flood- and spotlights
11 | table for still-life set-ups

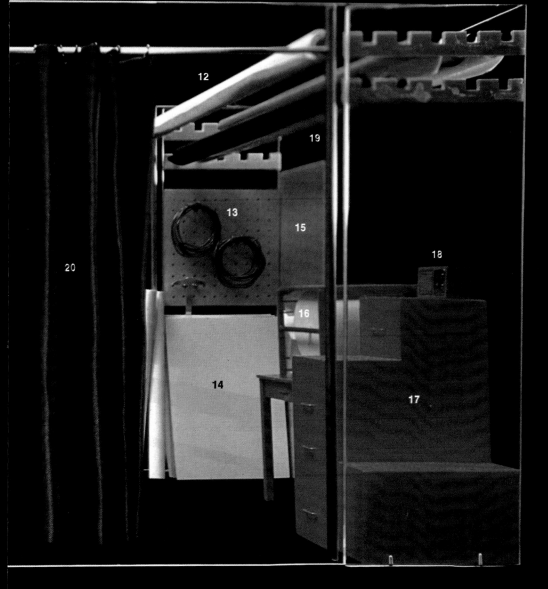

In a space no larger than a one-car garage, Al Freni has set up a studio, a scale model of which is shown at left. The entrance door is at far left. Next to it is a work desk with a light box for transparencies and a telephone. Drawers are underneath. Above the desk is a pegboard for masking tape and small tools. Above that: shelves for props as well as electronic-flash heads and reflectors. More shelves are next to the desk. An assortment of some of the lights Freni needs, together with all his electronic-flash power generators, is shown in the center of the picture. The rolls of seamless paper he often uses to make plain backgrounds are stored on handmade racks under the ceiling at far right. The space underneath is not wasted—it contains filing cabinets and a print dryer.

Every studio needs adjustable surface space for setting up still-life pictures. Freni has settled on a small draftsman's table whose top can be raised, lowered or tilted. If he wants more working surface he places on the table a large square of plywood that normally stands against a wall. For still larger surface he uses the floor.

Vital to his work are three movable "pole cat" poles; their ends are under spring pressure so that they wedge themselves securely between floor and ceiling anywhere they are placed in the room. They are located where they do not interfere with photography but can be used for clamping lights or reflectors, or for suspending a seamless paper backdrop. The two poles in the foreground are connected with a horizontal rod from which drapes can be hung to provide textured backgrounds.

12 seamless paper	18 radio
13 pegboard for extension cords	19 "pole cat" support poles
14 reflectors	20 black velvet curtain
15 door to darkroom	21 floodlight
16 print dryer	22 electronic-flash unit
17 storage cabinets	

Only 9 by 8—But a Complete Darkroom

In the model on the previous pages there is a door in the far right background. It is the same door shown here at right rear and leads to Freni's darkroom—a layout as economical of space as the studio.

The darkroom, though only nine by eight feet, is fully equipped for processing black-and-white negatives, also for making finished enlargements from them. The "wet" side for developing film and making prints is at the left in the specially constructed scale model shown opposite, with a large sink *(foreground)* that will hold two or three print trays and a wash tank. Under the sink are filing cabinet, wastebasket and storage space. Above are timers and a clothesline with pins for holding wet film and prints. Higher yet, and running all around the room, are shelves for chemicals, paper and other supplies. Along the far wall, next to the door, is a flat working surface with a paper cutter on it. Underneath are a filing cabinet and some vertical storage space. The near wall has another filing cabinet whose top Freni uses as a stand for his enlarger. The right wall is the "dry" side of the darkroom. Its flat work space has a refrigerator under it (Freni stores color film here, also ice cubes and the food products he photographs for advertising clients). Beyond the refrigerator is a lockable steel cabinet for storing cameras and lenses and an open area for hanging clothes. Air conditioning outlets are not shown; it is important that any darkroom be adequately ventilated, either by air conditioning or by fans, to dispel fumes.

1	entrance door from studio	9	storage cabinet
2	steel cabinet with lock for equipment storage	10	sink
3	storage shelves	11	print trays
4	refrigerator	12	timer
5	pegboard for tools	13	clothespins
6	enlarger	14	safelight
7	electric timer	15	folding table
8	enlarger easel	16	paper cutter

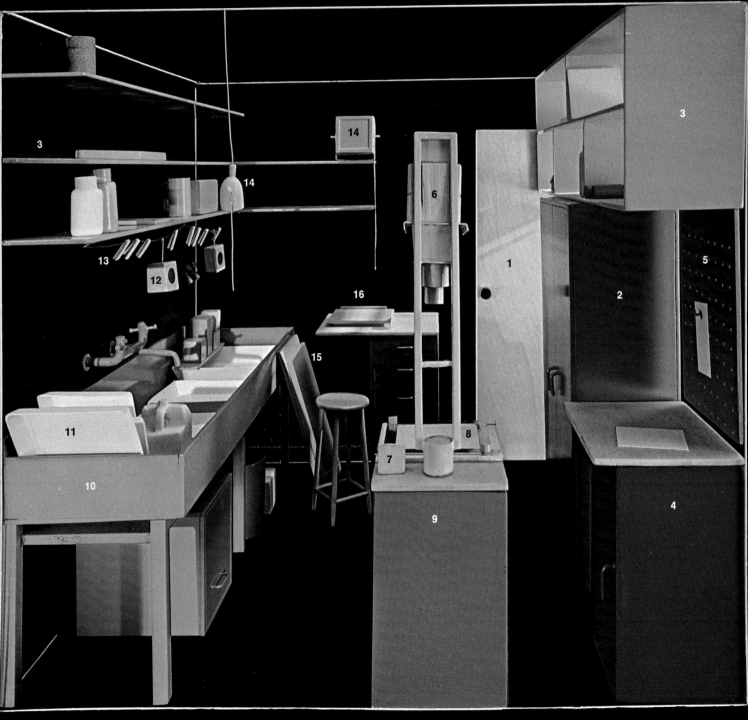

Squeezing a Big Picture into a Small Space

There are ways of making pictures that seem bigger than they are, even in small quarters. The photograph at right is a case in point. It was made by Al Freni in his studio to display knee-length sport socks.

Since the socks are sold for wear outdoors, Freni sought an outdoorsy look—so he rented a bicycle, artificial grass and some furniture. He wanted the girl's legs and the bicycle wheel to dominate his picture, and he could have done that fairly easily by using a wide-angle lens and shooting from a position close to the girl. This would have made the background props seem small and far away—as he desired —but that same wide angle would have pulled into the picture unwanted corners of the studio. A way had to be worked out to solve the background problem within walls that were only nine feet apart, and still preserve the illusion of space. To enhance this feeling of spaciousness he also wanted to make the background go just a little soft—a difficult effect to achieve with a wide-angle lens because of its great depth of field.

He solved both problems with a long-focal-length (150mm) lens on his 500C Hasselblad 2¼-inch-square camera. Its restricted depth of field slightly softened the background, and its limited angle of view eliminated the unwanted corners of the studio. All he needed now was the illusion of distance, and he achieved that by using miniature props. With a low camera angle, the table and chairs appear full size, and a respectable distance from the camera. Actually they are tiny, and only six feet behind the model, as the normal-lens shot on the opposite page reveals.

Small-scale props are the secret ingredient that gives a sense of space to a scene where space is actually missing. The table and chairs are children's garden furniture, the glasses are liqueur glasses, the "loaf" of bread a single hard roll, the bottle half the standard size. To achieve an effect of overall out-of-doors light with soft shadows, Freni bounced two electronic-flash lights off the studio walls and ceiling, and a third off an umbrella and reflecting card. The brief duration of the electronic flash's burst of light eliminated any possibility of motion blurring if his model did not hold still during the exposure.

The Darkroom Essentials

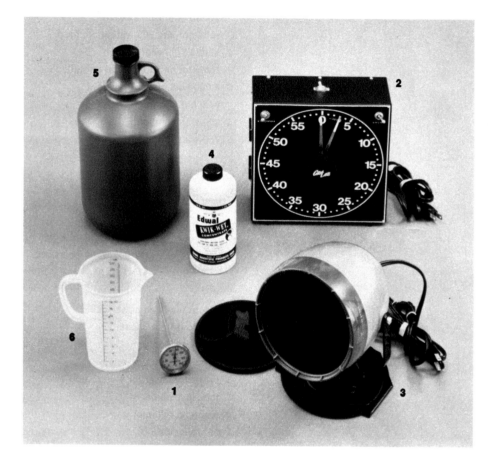

The basic darkroom shopping list includes the few standard items needed whether the film is small or large, roll or sheet, shown at left. Since film processing requires precise temperature control and timing, the list starts with a dependable thermometer and a timer. Also needed are a safelight with filters for adapting it to different film types; a bottle of wetting concentrate used in the drying of film to prevent water stains; several gallon jugs, like the one shown, for mixing chemicals, and a graduated beaker for measuring them. The chemicals are not shown.

To develop film, the photographer will need the items shown on the opposite page. He need not buy all the developing tanks shown—only those designed for the film sizes he uses, together with their respective hangers or reels. Besides, if he uses both 8 x 10 and 4 x 5 film, he can get by with only the larger tank, since his 4 x 5 film hangers will fit in it. Equipment used for printing varies widely, depending on studio needs, and is not shown. ☐

1 | thermometer
2 | electric timer, one second to one hour
3 | adjustable safelight lamp with filters
4 | wetting agent
5 | one-gallon opaque plastic jug (2 or 3 needed)
6 | 18-ounce measuring graduate

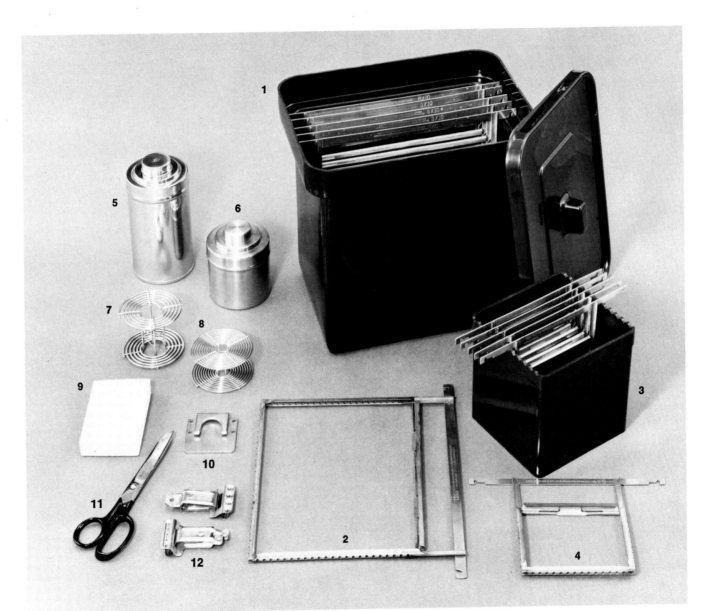

1 | 3½-gallon developing tank
and cover for 8 x 10 film
2 | stainless-steel 8 x 10
developing hanger
3 | 72-ounce developing tank for 4 x 5 film
4 | stainless-steel 4 x 5 developing hanger

5 | large stainless-steel developing tank
for roll film (holds two rolls of 120
size or four rolls of 35mm)
6 | small stainless-steel developing tank
for roll film (holds one roll of
120 or two rolls of 35mm)

7 | developing reel for 120 film
8 | developing reel for 35mm film
9 | sponge
10 | cassette opener
11 | scissors
12 | clips for holding wet film

A House That Doubles as a Workshop

Many photographers set aside a room at home as a studio. Bob Garrett, who does general portrait work in Columbus, Georgia, carried the idea to an extreme. He turned over almost all the ground floor and garden of his home to his studio operation to provide informal, homelike settings for his portraits.

Garrett had started out in downtown Columbus with a conventional studio; then, after a decade of experience there, he began hunting for something out of the ordinary: a suburban home with a garden that he could convert into his own photographic environment. He found it after about three years of looking, a lovely house with a magnificent garden, and closed up his studio downtown to open up at home.

Both house and garden have been exploited with great skill by Garrett to provide him with a variety of backgrounds. These backgrounds help him in three ways. First, they are right at hand, always ready; no time is wasted searching them out or setting them up. Second, he has used them over and over so many times that he knows exactly how to obtain the best from any of them. Third, they are tasteful—and real; they enable his subjects to feel casually at ease, while lending a style and conviction to his pictures that would be hard to find in a conventional studio.

The lower floor of the Garrett house, at first glance, resembles any finely appointed home. Actually it is almost all studio; he, his partner-wife and one daughter live upstairs. The large front hall is discreetly given over to a reception area. At one side is a handsome sweeping staircase. Since a large part of Garrett's business is photographing brides, this staircase is an invaluable prop for a bridal pose. Elsewhere on the ground floor are French doors, fireplaces with good andirons and well-proportioned mantels, arched and pedimented doorways of several designs and sizes, two or three different wallpaper patterns. All hint of elegant and gracious living and can be worked into Garrett's pictures as he or his clients think suitable. For more straightforward portraits, he has a conventional, strobe-lit working studio room with assorted hand-painted backgrounds.

Outdoors, the Garrett studio is even more remarkable. It consists of more than an acre of garden on three levels. The ground that slopes away from the house is a maze of brick and flagstone steps, ivy-covered walls, emerald-rich patches of grass and flowering borders. An Italianate fountain springs from a formal wall and splashes into a fish pool. There is also a waterfall that trickles down over a wall of heavy rocks to a little stream that ends in a lily pond. Spaciousness is provided by a flat stretch of open lawn with a gazebo at one side and some fine old trees to give a sense of permanence. Skillful planting of holly and other evergreen shrubs makes the garden useful all the year round. Anybody—business executive, bride, matron, family group—gains a gloss of instant aristocracy by being photographed in such a setting. Just about the only thing Garrett does not provide to serve as a background prop is a live Russian wolfhound. □

Bob Garrett's Home of Photography, which he runs with his wife, daughters and sons-in-law, is headquartered in this brick Georgian house. Downstairs are seven rooms given over to photography, as are the rear gardens, which came ready-made with the house (processing is done elsewhere). The bay window and French doors shown here can be used from inside as effective backdrops for portraits.

Even the narrow hallway (far left) leading from the foyer of Garrett's house to a display corridor contributes to the homelike atmosphere of his studio. It has delicately molded arches and an English-pattern wallpaper. The viewing and salesroom (left) has a framed easel onto which an opaque projector throws proofs of portraits for examination by customers.

For a photographer with a big bridal business a dressing room (far left) is a must. Garrett has an extremely comfortable one with a three-way dressing-table mirror. He lets his sitters apply their own makeup, checking only to see that it will photograph well. The picture at left shows one of the few nonauthentic setups Garrett uses: a prop corner in his working studio, where a leather chair and fake leather books create a setting for business portraits.

A bride-to-be poses for Garrett in her wedding gown, holding a prop bouquet from a selection that he keeps on the mantelpiece in the dressing room shown on the opposite page. Below at right the bride comes out into the hall for the inevitable staircase shot, while Garrett adjusts his lights and his daughter Sandra makes the folds of the train fall exactly into place.

Garrett's garden, which he was able to put to photographic use virtually unchanged, is rich in good settings: at top left a grassy walk edged with flagstones and evergreen shrubbery, at top right a formal gazebo with brick walk and garden table, at bottom left a graceful iron-railed flight of brick steps that doubles around a fountain and pool, and at bottom right a heavy rock wall with its own little waterfall.

For an informal sylvan portrait of a family that comes back each year to have a new picture taken, Garrett places the group against a background of trees in the garden's middle level. His daughter Sandra holds an umbrella reflector from which strobe light will be bounced to brighten in facial shadows. Behind the group the garden falls away into increasingly informal settings of winding paths and a lily pond.

Overleaf: Bob Garrett's daughter Jennie poses ▶ for her own bridal portrait in front of the waterfall at the Home of Photography.

BOB GARRETT: *Daughter Jennie as a Bride,* 1969

Coping with the Problems of Still Life 200

Shadows That Separate White from White 202
Tracing the Delicacy of Glassware 204
Keeping Ghosts out of Silverware 208
Catching the Freshness of Fruit 210

The Professional Approach 212

Fabrics in Close-Up 214
Fine Gems in Unusual Settings 216
Liquids in Suspension 218
Bringing Toys to Life 220
The Radiance of Flowers 222
Exploring the Beauty of Food 224
. . . Even the Kitchen Sink 230

IRVING PENN: *New York Still Life with Food*, 1947

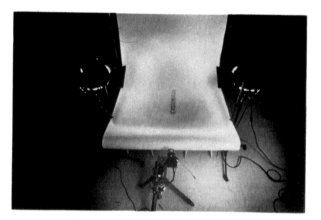

A colonnade of crystal (left) is softly backlighted by two large spotlights whose joined beams bounce off a sheet of seamless white paper, as shown above. The shadow that surrounds the bases of the glassware provides contrast with the brilliance cast by the reflected light source and lends an air of cool elegance to the photograph.

Two solid crystal figurines, a penguin and a porpoise, glow in the light of a pair of 200-watt spotlights covered with colored gelatin sheets. The spots were placed behind the translucent white seamless-paper backdrop (right), and the bright orange and blue beams they projected were narrowly confined by barn doors to bathe both penguin and porpoise in eerie hues.

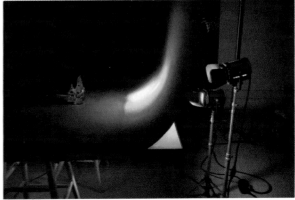

Keeping Ghosts out of the Silverware

Silver's mirrorlike qualities pose some unique problems. The highly polished pieces reflect every detail of their surroundings, a distracting trait when the surroundings include such irrelevant items as lights, photographer and camera. Sometimes reflections improve a picture, producing, as in the photograph at right, a bright and lively scene. The trick in either case is simply to move equipment around as necessary until none of it shows on the silver.

If, however, the reflective qualities of the silver must be reduced, two principal methods are available. Some photographers use matte spray, a special dulling agent that can be purchased in art-supply stores. But unless it is sparingly and cautiously used, the spray tends to produce flat, lifeless images. A better solution to the problem is a light tent like the one used for the white-on-white photographs on pages 202-203. It creates softly glowing but distraction-free pictures *(opposite)*.

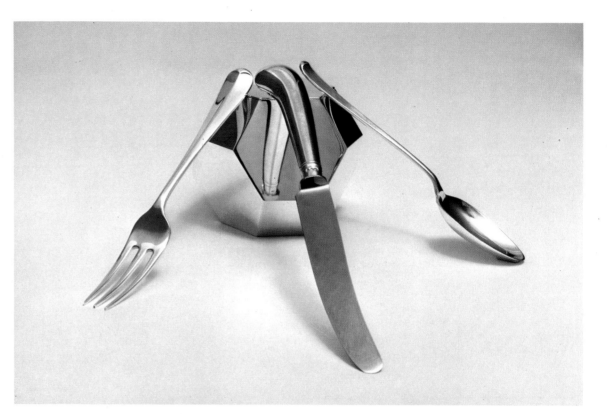

Partly enclosed in a red, white and blue housing (left), brightly polished sterling flatware and a box acquire a striped tricolor pattern (above). A brilliant Sungun floodlight was directed at the housing ceiling, subduing and scattering the light so that the silver mirrored the colors of the sides.

To minimize distracting reflections on an artful arrangement of sterling, an extra length of fiberglass was draped over the front of the photographer's light tent (right), a small opening being left for the camera lens. The subtly highlighted patterns of reflection were created by aiming the Sungun at an angled paper screen to the right of the camera. The reflected light was then diffused by the walls of the tent.

Catching the Freshness of Fruit

Each photographer develops his own favorite tricks for making fruit and vegetables glisten and appear fresh and appetizing. Some professionals use a dropper or paint brush to apply glycerine or glycerine mixtures to the food; the viscous liquid clings to the surface of the fruit and gives the impression of dewlike moisture. Alternatively, mineral oil may be applied in a thin layer to a vegetable or a piece of fruit, providing a surface on which drops of water will collect. In the center picture at right, still a third technique was employed: mist from a household spray bottle filled with water provided just the right amount of wetness.

With such tricks some form of backlighting is preferred, since it silhouettes the droplets, adding dimension to the surface texture of the fruit. The light almost always comes from electronic-flash equipment. Unlike hot floodlights, which will dry out and discolor vegetables or fruit and dissolve ice cream or aspics, the powerful flash units deliver their bursts of intense light so briefly that the food is not affected. □

Conveying the desired effect of moisture and freshness, juicy halves of fruit (above) glisten under light reflected from an umbrella placed over an electronic flash positioned almost directly above the subject (left). Since it shows no shadows, the black paper background concentrates attention on the rough pulpy texture of the fruit.

A close-up study of rough-textured oranges, smooth-skinned apples and a single grape (above) is enhanced by backlighted water droplets applied to the fruit with a spray bottle. An electronic flash with a fiberglass diffuser faces the fruit and its black backdrop, while another flash unit towers over the arrangement from the rear to provide the necessary backlighting (right).

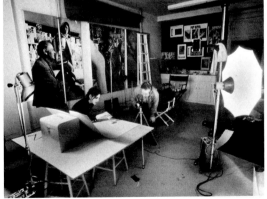

Suspended over a lemon half, a delicate, pearl-like drop of juice emphasizes the succulence of the fruit and even manages to convey a sense of tartness. The effect was created with two electronic-flash units: one, a fill-in light at the camera's left, was directed into an umbrella, and the other, partly shielded by a piece of cardboard, served as the predominating backlight.

The Professional Approach

At its best, a picture of an object is a still life in the classic sense: a work of art that, in revealing the character of the subject, arouses fresh appreciation of its qualities. This high goal is the aim of the professional studio photographer. How well he achieves it—despite unusual limitations on his artistic freedom—can be seen on these and the following pages. Only occasionally can he choose his subject matter and work with such traditional objects as flowers or fruit. More often he must create to order an image of beauty from commercial products or other objects that are infrequently associated with serious works of art—a pot, an electric lighting fixture, a piece of cloth.

To promote a line of earthenware, Henry Sandbank, a New York photographer, spent several days juxtaposing various items, searching for an austere but esthetically pleasing combination of shapes, sizes and colors. His final shot, strongly sidelighted, dramatically utilizes color, light and shadow.

The picture on the opposite page is the work of Aldo Ballo, a former architecture student who specializes in interpreting the avant-garde industrial design for which his native Milan is renowned. His photograph, commissioned by a Milanese furniture firm, clearly defines the lamp and table, but includes a pattern of reflections that makes it an effective object-portrait.

Brilliant lighting accentuates the shiny surfaces of a coffeepot and jug. A 1,000-watt flood was set to the left of the subjects while two angled pieces of white cardboard—one only slightly larger than the jug, the other slightly smaller—were placed out of camera range at the right and at the rear to guide a minimal reflection around to the right side, defining the shape of the earthenware.

HENRY SANDBANK: *Earthenware Utensils with a Spoon,* 1967

Surface sheen characterizes the red plastic of this lamp and table, illuminated from one side by two 900-watt banks of floodlights. The lamp was suspended only a foot above the tabletop in order to place it near the center of the frame, and a plate of dried fruit was so placed as to relieve the severe lines of the molded plastic objects.

ALDO BALLO: *Molded Plastic Furniture*, 1969

Fabrics in Close-up

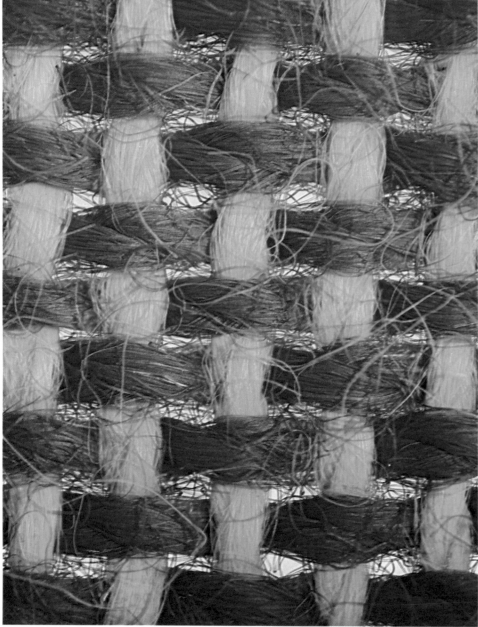

MANFRED KAGE: *Orlon magnified 20X, here enlarged to 45X, 1969*

At first glance the two pictures on these pages seem to bear no resemblance. They show different things and were made by different photographers using radically different techniques. And yet both achieve the same purpose: they convey the idea of fabric without showing fabric as it is ordinarily seen.

For the greatly enlarged view of Orlon at left, Manfred Kage set up an optical bench: a guide rail to which he attached a small lamp to backlight the fabric, a condenser lens to focus the light, a filter, the fabric sample and a view camera. The subtly colored remnants of thread in the composition at right were photographed by John Ellard in an English mill. Meticulously framing the subject with his 35mm camera, manipulating it and the lighting angle, he achieved a result as precisely controlled as Kage's.

Many times larger than life, this photomacrograph of an Orlon swatch was backlighted so that wispy dark strands of thread would be clearly visible. Frontlighting made the light-colored strands show up and revealed the pattern of the weave.

The balls of thread at right look like yarn from grandmother's knitting basket but are "thrums" —waste from the warp section of a loom. Daylight from a nearby window illuminated them.

JOHN ELLARD: *Warp Waste in a Spinning Factory*, 1969

Fine Gems in Unusual Settings

Jewelry is a most difficult subject to photograph effectively. It can be as transparent as glass and as full of reflections as silverware or cut crystal, posing a complex of problems. Small and delicate, jewelry must be photographed with utmost precision to reveal the details of workmanship. Usually it is shown in life-sized, or greater-than-life-sized, close-ups, adding to the difficulty of producing needle-sharp pictures —the closer the camera to the subject, the more restricted the depth of field and the smaller the area of sharp focus. Cut gems are particularly demanding subjects. Since their brilliance comes from the way light glints across their facets, the photographer must adjust his lighting to make as many facets glow as possible. In addition, the photographer faces the challenge of finding imaginative props to set off the jewelry's richness and elegance.

Photographers often cope with the technical difficulties of gem photography by setting up the jewels inside a light tent *(page 202),* and carefully balancing the illumination with spotlights and flood lamps. To preserve sharp focus within a limited depth of field, they usually keep the center of interest of the composition within a single plane, as in the arrangement of brooches and pendants at right. Individual photographers have discovered certain finer points of composition and lighting for themselves, and are sometimes reluctant to reveal their hard-earned formulas. Charles Collum, who made the red diamond in the coconut half glow so brilliantly on the opposite page, refuses to say exactly how he did it. "That," he declares, "would be giving away my best trade secret."

CHARLES R. COLLUM: *Arrangement with Opals,* 1969

An antique nutmeg grater provides an unusual foil for a sparkling display of opal jewelry set with cut diamonds and other gems (above). For maximum clarity, the photographer placed all the gems at the same distance from his 8 x 10 view camera. The same photographer used a coconut half to give an exotic air to his picture of a red diamond (opposite, bottom). The shaggy husk and white meat contrast with the precisely cut gem.

Fresh vegetables, according to Fred Burrell, who ▶ photographed the two brooches with tomato and artichoke slices (top right), make an ideal setting for jewelry. Fleshy, moist and alive, they set off the hardness of stone and metal. Burrell placed each vegetable, sliced paper thin, on a white translucent panel inside a light tent. Each brooch, laid on top of its vegetable slice, was lighted from below with a small spot and from above with two flood lamps and was photographed with a 4 x 5 view camera stopped down to f/22.

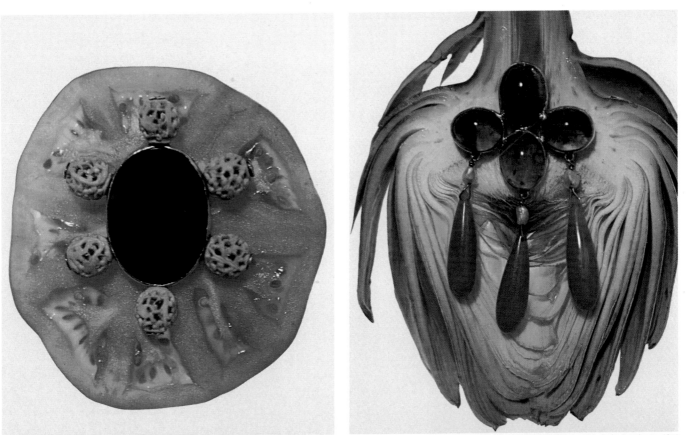

FRED BURRELL: *Brooch of Onyx and Carved Ivory*, 1968

FRED BURRELL: *Brooch of Amethysts with Jade Pendants*, 1968

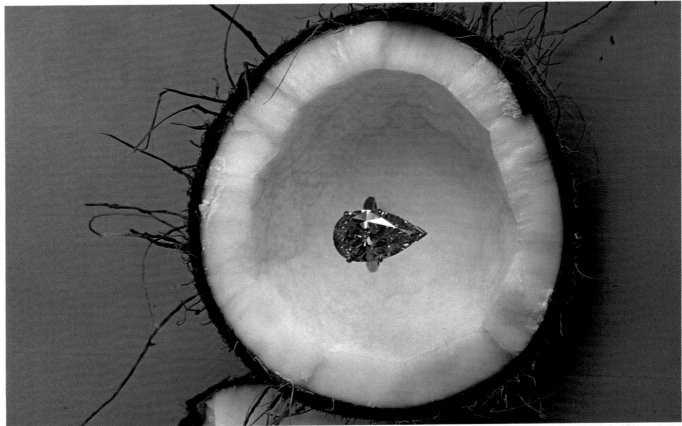

CHARLES R. COLLUM: *Red Diamond*, 1969

The Art in Everyday Objects: continued

Liquids in Suspension

A Leitz Aristophot, an elaborate close-up apparatus, allowed the photographer to catch this strange magnified view of a blue-dyed drop of water poised near the edge of a nylon curtain. Since the curtain was water repellent, he had ample time to experiment with lighting, subject and camera angles. He placed the drop on the curtain edge, beneath the lens of the Aristophot. Two floodlights, equipped with heat-absorbing glass filters to guard against evaporation, illuminated the subject from above. A small spotlight aimed at an angled mirror below the material provided backlighting to define the sharp edges of warp, woof and water droplet.

A sleek spout of champagne, highlighted by the ▶ reflected illumination of two electronic-flash units, cascades into a pool of bubbles. The flash units, placed symmetrically on either side of the camera, were essential for stopping the motion of the pouring champagne. To eliminate shadows and distracting reflections, the photographer isolated the glass and bottle against a black velvet background. Choosing to accentuate bubbles rather than bottle in shooting this photograph for a champagne advertisement, he shielded the foil-wrapped neck of the bottle by placing pieces of cardboard between the lights and the upper part of the setup.

MANFRED KAGE: *Water Drop on a Curtain*, 1970

RETO BERNHARDT: *Advertisement for Champagne,* 1963

BERT STERN: *Bread and Wine,* 1953

The ingredients of a classically simple meal
—a loaf of bread and a bottle of wine—are served
up as the main elements of a meticulously
balanced design. The photographer arranged the
bottle to complement the dark, vertical cylinder of
the table base; the horizontal line of the tabletop
is reinforced by the knife blade jutting in from the
left. The folds of the napkin not only hide the
support that keeps the knife in place, but also
echo the curved shape of the bread.

The milk is as unappetizing as chalk, and the fried ▶
egg looks as hard and shiny as china, but this
picture, with its strong patterns and strange
perspectives, is immensely powerful. "By pure
design and composition," notes the
photographer, "I was able to create a surrealistic
photograph using these generic food objects."
He suspended his view camera above the table,
but slightly ahead of its forward edge, to take the
picture from an angle rather than from squarely
overhead. A single spotlight was located below
the camera to cast the dark shadows of the bottle
and glass against the light backboard.

HENRY SANDBANK: *Egg and Milk*, 1968

PETE TURNER: *Cruets with a Lemon*, 1968

These two esthetic compositions were created from the commonest of objects, but with totally different techniques. Pete Turner arranged the one above with painstaking care: he filled a cruet with red vinegar, stoppered it tightly, upended it, and rested a lemon on its base. He then filled another cruet with olive oil, put a sprig of tarragon in it, and suspended it above the lemon. An electronic flash, poised overhead, shone through the oil-filled cruet to deepen the yellow of the lemon; another flash, aimed at white cardboard in the background, silhouetted the fruit.

By contrast, Gene Laurents' picture *(opposite)* is the result of patient observation. Living in Paris, he noticed that the proprietor of a restaurant regularly displayed fresh fruit behind an etched-glass window. Laurents kept watching until the day when the arrangement was precisely to his liking, and shot his picture at twilight to give it a purplish cast.

GENE LAURENTS: *Pears in a Paris Window,* 1961

. . . Even the Kitchen Sink

A kitchen sink? Yes, even such utilitarian hardware can be a still life, and possibly a beautiful one. Lynn St. John proves the point by artful use of lighting in this picture, made as an advertisement for kitchen plumbing.

St. John faced all the usual problems encountered when photographing reflective surfaces—in this case, chrome and enamel. He solved them by illuminating his subject with two electronic-flash units bounced off a white board placed in front of the sink at an angle of 45°. This left the foreground portion of the faucets in shadow. To give shape to the polished enamel interior of the sink, he pasted black strips onto the white board, placed to prevent light from reflecting off parts of its bottom and sides. The cool, modeled beauty of the result seems as sleek and efficient as the control console of a sports car —and as arresting as a specimen of contemporary sculpture.   ☐

LYNN ST. JOHN: *Kitchen Sink*, 1967

Bibliography

Avedon, Richard, and Truman Capote, *Observations*. Simon & Schuster, 1959.
Ballard, Bettina, *In My Fashion*. David McKay, 1960.
Beaton, Cecil:
The Glass of Fashion. Doubleday, 1954.
The Wandering Years. Little, Brown, 1961.
Blum, Daniel, *A Pictorial History of the Silent Screen*. Grosset & Dunlap, 1953.
Chase, Edna Woolman, and Ilka Chase, *Always in Vogue*. Doubleday, 1954.
Giebelhausen, Joachim, ed., *Manual of Applied Photography*. Verlag Grossbild-Technik, 1966.
Horst, Horst P., *Photographs of a Decade*. J. J. Augustin, 1962.
Levin, Phyllis Lee, *The Wheels of Fashion*. Doubleday, 1965.
MacGowan, Kenneth, *Behind the Screen*. Delacorte, 1965.
Newhall, Beaumont, *The History of Photography*. The Museum of Modern Art, 1964.
Penn, Irving, *Moments Preserved*. Simon & Schuster, 1960.
Pollack, Peter, *The Picture History of Photography*. Harry N. Abrams, 1958.
Ray, Man, *Man Ray, Self Portrait*. Little, Brown, 1963.
Snow, Carmel, with Mary Louise Aswell, *The World of Carmel Snow*. McGraw-Hill, 1962.
Stroebel, Leslie, *View Camera Techniques*. Hastings House, 1967.
Taft, Robert, *Photography and the American Scene*. Dover, 1938.
Taylor, Deems, *A Pictorial History of the Movies*. Simon & Schuster, 1943.
Trahey, Jane, ed., *Harper's Bazaar, 100 Years of the American Female*. Random House, 1967.
Wahl, Paul, *Press/View Camera Technique*. American Photographic Book Publishing, 1969.

Magazines

Aperture, Aperture Inc., New York City.
British Journal of Photography, Henry Greenwood and Co., London.
Camera, C. J. Bucher Ltd., Lucerne, Switzerland.
Camera 35, U.S. Camera Publishing Co., New York City.
Creative Camera, International Federation of Amateur Photographers, London.
Famous Photographers Magazine, Westport, Connecticut.
Harper's Bazaar, Hearst Magazines, Inc., New York City.
Holiday, Holiday Publishing Co., Indianapolis.
Infinity, American Society of Magazine Photographers, New York City.
Modern Photography, The Billboard Publishing Co., New York City.
Popular Photography, Ziff-Davis Publishing Co., New York City.
Travel & Camera, U.S. Camera Publishing Corp., New York City.
U.S. Camera World Annual, U.S. Camera Publishing Corp., New York City.
Vogue, The Condé Nast Publications Inc., New York City.

Acknowledgments

For assistance in the preparation of this volume, the editors thank the following individuals, collections and firms: Mehemed Fehmy Agha, Malvern, Pennsylvania; Jerry Arena, Production Manager, Color Unlimited, Inc., New York City; Richard Avedon, New York City; Paul Bonner, The Condé Nast Publications Inc., New York City; Zenja Cary, Cary Kitchens, New York City; Walter Clark, Rochester, New York; F. Van Deren Coke, Deputy Director, Eastman House, Rochester, New York; Arnold Crane, Chicago, Illinois; George Cukor, Hollywood, California; Louise Dahl-Wolfe, Frenchtown, New Jersey; Louise Effron, New York City; Bea Feitler, Art Director, *Harper's Bazaar*, New York City; Ludovico Ferraglio, Ferraglio-Newbery Associates, Inc., New York City; Al Freni, New York City; George Fry, Manager, Electronic Flash Department, Willoughby's, New York City; Stanley Glaubach, New York City; Lowell Hocking, Director, Jacksonville Museum, Jacksonville, Oregon; Max Keizerstein, Manager, Studio Equipment, Willoughby's, New York City; T. J. Le Comte, Sinar Product Manager, Ehrenreich Photo-Optical Industries, Inc., Garden City, Long Island, New York; Phyllis Lee Levin, The Condé Nast Publications Inc., New York City; Eaton S. Lothrop, Jr., Editor, *Photographic Collectors' Newsletter*, Brooklyn, New York; Yvonne McHarg, New York City; Tomas Newbery, Ferraglio-Newbery Associates, Inc., New York City; Irving Penn, New York City; Charles Reiser, Professional, Commercial and Industrial Markets Division, Eastman Kodak Company, Rochester, New York; John H. Reynolds, National News Director, University of Southern California, Los Angeles, California; Hal Siegman, General Manager, Horn/Griner Studio, New York City; Harry Warnecke, New York City.

Picture Credits

Credits from left to right are separated by semicolons, from top to bottom by dashes.

COVER: Ken Kay

Chapter 1: 11—Edward Steichen, courtesy Museum of Modern Art, New York. 20—© Karsh of Ottawa from Rapho Guillumette. 21—© Arnold Newman. 22, 23—Harris & Ewing from Gilloon Photo Agency. 24, 25—Richard Avedon, copyright © 1970 The Condé Nast Publications Inc. 26—Roddy McDowall. 27—© Barbara Morgan. From *Martha Graham,* Duell, Sloan & Pearce, 1940. 28, 29—© Philippe Halsman. 30 —Melvin Sokolsky, courtesy *Harper's Bazaar.* 31 —Guy Bourdin, courtesy *Harper's Bazaar.* 32 —Ylla from Rapho Guillumette. 33—Norman Wightman. 34—Irving Penn, copyright © 1948 The Condé Nast Publications Inc. 35—© Toni Frissell for LIFE, courtesy Library of Congress. 36—Milton Halberstadt. 37—Nob Fukuda from Photo Trends. 38—Henry Sandbank, courtesy Wells, Rich, Greene. 39—Peter Scolamiero. 40 —Ernst Haas, courtesy Volkswagen. 41—Hiro, courtesy Cowles Syndicate. 42—Lionel Freedman.

Chapter 2: 45—Courtesy Anna C. Gossner. 48, 49 —Evelyn Hofer, courtesy Jacksonville Museum, Jacksonville, Oregon. 50, 51—Evelyn Hofer, courtesy Henry Ford Museum and Greenfield Village. 52—T. C. Marceau, copied by Paulus Leeser, courtesy Eastman Kodak Company. 53 —Copied by Paulus Leeser, courtesy Eastman Kodak Company. 54 through 57—Culver Pictures. 58—Wilton Tifft; drawing by Herbert H. Quarmby. 59—Wilton Tifft; courtesy *Daily News.* 60, 61, 62—John Senzer. 63—Rudy Muller. 64, 65, 66—Wilton Tifft. 67—Lionel Freedman. 68 —Photographs by Heinz Kluetmeier; drawing by Herbert H. Quarmby. 69—Pohlman Studios. 70 through 76—Wilton Tifft.

Chapter 3: 79—John Senzer, courtesy Horn/Griner Studio. 89—Y. R. Okamoto, courtesy Lyndon Baines Johnson Library. 90, 91—© Arnold Newman. 92—Louise Dahl-Wolfe. 93 —Louise Dahl-Wolfe, courtesy *Harper's Bazaar.* 94, 95, 96—John Senzer. 97—John Senzer; Rudy Muller. 99—Keith Trumbo for Irving Penn Studios. 100—Per Boije for Irving Penn Studios. 101—Irving Penn, copyright © 1967 The Condé Nast Publications Inc. 102—Irving Penn, copyright © 1970 The Condé Nast Publications Inc.

Chapter 4: 105—Edward Steichen, courtesy Museum of Modern Art, New York. 108—Baron de Meyer, copied by Paulus Leeser from *Camera Work,* courtesy Museum of Modern Art, New York. 109—Top left, Baron de Meyer, copyright © 1921 The Condé Nast Publications Inc.—Baron de Meyer, courtesy Louise Dahl-Wolfe and George Eastman House (2). 110, 111 —Edward Steichen, courtesy Museum of Modern Art, New York. 112—George Hoyningen-Huene, copyright © 1931 The Condé Nast Publications Inc., courtesy Horst. 113—George Hoyningen-Huene, copyright © The Condé Nast Publications Inc., courtesy Horst. 114—Cecil Beaton, copyright © 1934 The Condé Nast Publications Inc. 115—Cecil Beaton, copyright © 1949 The Condé Nast Publications Inc.; Cecil Beaton, copyright © 1937 The Condé Nast Publications Inc. (3). 116, 117—Man Ray, courtesy *Harper's Bazaar.* 118, 119—Martin Munkacsi, courtesy *Harper's Bazaar* and Joan Munkacsi Hammes. 120—Toni Frissell, courtesy *Harper's Bazaar* and Library of Congress. 121 —Toni Frissell, copyright © 1938 The Condé Nast Publications Inc. 122, 123—Louise Dahl-Wolfe, courtesy *Harper's Bazaar.* 124—Horst. 125—Horst, copyright © 1937 The Condé Nast Publications Inc. 126, 127—Irving Penn, copyright © 1947 The Condé Nast Publications Inc.; Irving Penn, copyright © 1950 The Condé Nast Publications Inc. 128—Richard Avedon. 129 —Richard Avedon, copyright © 1968 The Condé Nast Publications Inc. 131—Melvin Sokolsky, courtesy *Harper's Bazaar.* 132, 133—Hiro, courtesy *Harper's Bazaar;* Art Kane. 134, 135 —Silano, courtesy *Harper's Bazaar.* 136 —Alberto Rizzo, courtesy *Harper's Bazaar.* 137 —Bert Stern. 138—Art Kane, copyright © 1963 The Condé Nast Publications Inc. 139—Creative Team, Ulrich & Fehlman, Zurich. 140—Alen MacWeeney.

Chapter 5: 143—Ken Kay. 145—Drawing by Nicholas Fasciano. 146 through 170—Ken Kay. 158—Caucasian design rug courtesy A. Beshar Co., New York. 160, 161—Hôtel de Varengeville, Wrightman Galleries, Metropolitan Museum of Art. 170—Bird by Lalique for Nina Ricci Parfums, courtesy Jacqueline Cochran, Inc.

Chapter 6: 173—Courtesy Robert E. Cunningham. 176 through 179—Models by Nicholas Fasciano, photographs by Neal Slavin. 180 through 189—Al Freni. 180, 181—Properties courtesy F.A.O. Schwarz and RMH International, Inc. 190 through 195—John Senzer. 196—Robert Garrett.

Chapter 7: 199—Irving Penn, copyright © 1947 The Condé Nast Publications Inc. 202 through 211—Erich Hartmann from Magnum. 202, 203 —China courtesy RMH International, Inc. 207 —Crystal courtesy Steuben Glass. 208, 209 —Silver courtesy Tiffany & Company. 212 —Henry Sandbank. 213—Aldo Ballo. 214, 215 —Manfred Kage from Peter Arnold; John Ellard. 216—Charles R. Collum, courtesy Glenn Advertising for Fine Jewelers Guild. 217—Fred Burrell (2)—Charles R. Collum, courtesy Glenn Advertising for Fine Jewelers Guild. 218 —Manfred Kage from Peter Arnold. 219—Reto Bernhardt, courtesy Gerstner, Gredinger & Kutter, Basel. 220, 221—Paul Caponigro; © Thomas Cugini, courtesy H. P. His, Basel. 222, 223, 224—Paul Caponigro. 225—B. Truttman, courtesy Alan Porter, *Camera Magazine,* Lucerne. 226—© 1971 Bert Stern. 227—Henry Sandbank. 228—© Pete Turner. 229—Gene Laurents. 230—Lynn St. John.

Index
Numerals in italics indicate a photograph, painting or drawing of the subject mentioned.

Agha, Mehemed Fehmy, 107, 124
American Home magazine, 61, 62
Anderson, Marian, 16
Animals, photography of, *32-33*
Architecture, photography of, with view camera, *164-165, 166-167*
Art, influence of, on fashion photography, 130
Avedon, Doe, 14
Avedon, Richard, 70; biography and method of, 13-17; fashion photography of, 128; photographs by, *24-25, 128-129*

Backdrops, projected, *68*
Backlighting, *202, 204-205, 206-207, 210, 211, 214, 218, 222-223*
Ballo, Aldo, 212; photograph by, *213*
Barn doors, *187*, 201; and lighting technique, *203, 204, 206-207*
Beaton, Cecil, 106, 112, 114; photographs by, *114-115;* quoted, 106, 113
Bellows: bag, 144, *158;* extensions for photomacrography, *168*
Bendel, Henri, 115
Bernhardt, Reto, photograph by, *219*
Bitzer, Billy, 56
Bourdin, Guy, photograph by, *31*
Brady, Mathew, studio of, *47*
Britt, Peter, 49; portrait studio of, *48-49*
Brodovitch, Alexey, biography of, 16
Burrell, Fred, 216; photographs by, *217*
Burton, Richard, 128

Camera(s): for color, *58;* motorized, *182;* 2¼ x 2¼ single-lens reflex, *183;* 35mm single-lens reflex, *182;* for tintypes, *50;* 4 x 5 view camera, *184;* 8 x 10 view camera, *185*. See also View camera
Camera-backs: motorized, *182;* Polaroid, *183, 184;* revolving, *185*
Caponigro, Paul, 222; photographs by, *220, 222-223, 224*
Carbon arc, *56-57*
Carnegie, Hattie, 125
Cartier-Bresson, Henri, 13
Cary, Zenja, and job of home economist, 86
Chanel, Gabrielle, 112, *124*
Chase, Ilka, 115
Children, photography of, *34-35*
Classic Displays Incorporated (CDI), *70-76*
Colette, 18
Collum, Charles R., 216; photographs by, *216, 217*
Color: in fashion photography, *122-123;* studio for, *58-59*
Commercial photography, *36, 38-42, 47, 60-76;* of food, *60-63;* general product, *36, 38-42, 68-69;* large studio operations, 80-87; of room settings, *70-76;* sets for, *70-76;* and specialization within the studio, 80-87. See also Fashion photography; Still-life

photography
Condé Nast Publications Inc., 107, 108
Coolidge, Calvin, 22, *23*
Courrèges, André, 136
Crawford, Frances, *60*
Cugini, Thomas, photograph by, *220-221*

Daguerre, Louis, 46
Daguerrean Journal, 47
Dahl-Wolfe, Louise, 123; on location, 88, *92;* photographs by, *92, 93, 122-123*
Dali, Salvador, *28-29*
Darkroom: equipment for, *188-189;* and home studio, 178, *179*
De Meyer, Gayne, 106, 108; photographs by, *108-109*
De Mille, Cecil B., 56
Depth of field, and view camera movements, *158*
Diffusion screen, *183*
Distortion, and view camera movements, *159, 164-165.* See also Shape
Draper, John W., studio of, 46

Eagels, Jeanne, *109*
Effron, Louise, and job as a stylist, 83-84
Eisenhower, Dwight D., 23
Electronic-flash lighting, 186, *187;* and animal photography, 32; and lighting technique, 200; and still-life photography, *210-211,* 219, 228, 230
Ellard, John, 214; photograph by, *215*
Elle magazine, 138
Equipment: for darkroom, 178, *179, 188-189;* for 2¼ x 2¼ single-lens reflex camera, *183;* for 35mm single-lens reflex camera, *182;* for studio, 175, *176-177, 186-187;* for 4 x 5 view camera, *184;* for 8 x 10 view camera, *185.* See also Camera(s)
Ewing, Martha, 22
Extension rings, *183*

Fabrics, photography of, *214-215*
Fashion photography, *105,* 106-107, *108-140;* evolution of, *108-129;* introduction of color, *122-123;* introduction of sex, 138; modern, *130-140;* purpose of, 106
Film size, and lens design, *146-147*
Filter(s): heat-absorbing, 218; for 35mm single-lens reflex camera, *182;* for view cameras, *184, 185*
Flood lamps: early use of, 56; and lighting technique, 200, *202-203, 208-209,* 212, 213, 216, 218; photofloods, 186, *187;* quartz floodlights, 186, *187*
Flowers, photography of, *222-223*
Focus: and emphasis, 162, *163;* and swing of lens, 154, *155;* and tilt of lens, 152, *153*
Fonssagrives, Lisa, 19, *126*
Food, photography of, *60-63,* 86, *210-211, 224-229*
Franklin, Evelyn, 14

Freedgood, Martin, 70
Freedman, Lionel, 42, *64;* photographs by, *42, 67;* studio of, *64-67*
Freni, Al, studio of, 174-175, *176-181*
Frissell, Toni, 120; photographs by, *35, 120-121*
Front-projection system, *68*
Fukuda, Nob, 36; photograph by, *37*

Galanos, James, 130
Garrett, Bob, *193, 195;* photograph by, *196;* studio of, 190-196. See also Home of Photography
Garrett, Jennie, *196*
Gelatins, in lighting, *184, 185, 207*
Giuffrido-Ruggeri, Elisabetta Cristina, *34*
Glass, photography of, *204-207, 228-229*
Glaubach, Stanley, 82
Goldwyn, Samuel, 56
Graham, Martha, 26, *27*
Griffith, D. W., 56
Griner, Norman, 87

Haas, Ernst, 40; photograph by, *40*
Halberstadt, Milton, photograph by, *36*
Halsman, Philippe: creation of *Dali Atomicus, 28;* photographs by, *28-29;* quoted, 13
Hand, Learned, 18
Harding, Warren G., 22
Harper's Bazaar magazine, 12, 15, 16, 92, 107, 116, 118, 120, 130
Harris, George W., 22
Harris & Ewing, 22
Hartmann, Erich, demonstration of still-life photography, *202-211*
Henry Ford Museum, 50
Hepburn, Katharine, quoted, 112
Hiro, 16, 40, 132; photographs by, *41, 132;* quoted, 130
Hoffman, Dustin, 86
Holler, Henry, 44
Home economists, 86
Home of Photography, *190-191;* variety of indoor settings, *192-193;* variety of outdoor settings, *194-195*
Hoover, Herbert, 23
Horn, Steve, 80
Horn/Griner Studio, 78-83, 87
Horst, H. P., 124; photographs by, *124-125;* quoted, 124
Hoyningen-Huene, George, 107, 112; photographs by, *112-113;* quoted, 112

Jaffry, Jacques, *60*
Jesse Lasky Feature Play Company, 54
Jewelry, photography of, *216-217*
Johnson, Lyndon B., 89

Kage, Manfred, 214; photographs by, *214, 218*
Kane, Art, 132, 138; photographs by, *133, 138*
Karsh, Yousuf, 20; photograph by, *20*
Kay, Ken, 170; photographs by, *cover, 143, 146-170*
Kennedy, John F., 23

Lasky, Jesse, 54
Laurents, Gene, 228; photograph by, *229*
Leigh, Dorian, 13
Lens(es): design and film size, *146-147;* for 2¼ x 2¼ single-lens reflex camera, *183;* for 35mm single-lens reflex camera, *182;* for 4 x 5 view camera, *184;* for 8 x 10 view camera, *185*
Lewis, John L., 20
Liberman, Alexander, 18
Light table, 201
Light tent, 201, *202-203, 208-209,* 216
Lighting: in early studios, 46, 50, 54; introduction of artificial, 56; and still-life photography, 200-201, *202-211,* 212-215, 216, 218, 220, 222, 224, 226, 228, 230; types of equipment for, 186, *187*
Lighting techniques, 200-201; for fabrics, *214-215,* 218; for flowers, *222-223;* for food, *210-211,* 224, 226, 228; for glass, *204-207, 228;* for jewelry, *216-217;* for liquids, *211, 219;* for metals, *208-209,* 230; for toys, *220;* for white objects on a white background, *202-203*
Lights, studio, 186, *187;* stands for, *187.* See also Lighting
Liquids, photography of, *211, 219*
Location, studio photography on: by Louise Dahl-Wolfe, 88, *92-93;* by Arnold Newman, 88, *90-91;* by Rudy Muller, *94-97;* by Irving Penn, 88, 98, *99-102*
Loren, Sophia, *24-25*
Luna, Donyale, *128*

McDowall, Roddy, 26; photograph by, *26*
McHarg, Yvonne, and job of stylist, 84-86
MacWeeney, Alen, 140; photograph by, *140*
Marceau, Theodore C., studio, *52-53*
Marin, John, 18
Matte spray, 208
Morehouse, Marion, *110*
Morgan, Barbara, 26; photograph by, *27*
Morse, Samuel F. B., studio of, 46
Movements, view camera, 144; and depth of field, *158;* and distortion, *159, 164-165;* and elimination of unwanted objects in picture, *160-161;* and illusion of movement, *170;* rise and fall of back, *148-149;* rise and fall of front, *148-149;* and selection of emphasis, *162-163;* shift of back, *150-151;* shift of front, *150-151;* and still lifes, *156-157;* swing of back, *154-155;* swing of front, *154-155;* tilt of back, *152-153;* tilt of front, *152-153*
Movie studios: and artificial lighting, 56; early, *54-55, 56-57*
Muhlemann, H. P., 138; photograph by, *139*
Muller, Rudy, 61, *62;* on location, *94-97;* photographs by, *63, 97;* studio of, *60-63*
Munkacsi, Martin, 118; photographs by, *118-119*

235

Newman, Arnold, 20; on location, 88, 90; photographs by, *21, 90, 91*
Nichols, Mike, 128
Nilsson, Birgit, *26*
Noguchi, Isamu, 20, *21*
Norell, Norman, quoted, 130
Nowell, Dorcas, 14

Parker, Suzy, 13, 128
Patchet, Jean, *127*
Penn, Arthur, 18
Penn, Irving, 12, 13, 16, 127, 138, 200; biography and method of, 17-19; fashion photography of, 127; on location, 88, 98, *99-102*; photographs by, *34, 101, 102, 126-127, 199;* studio photography by, 200
Pets, photography of, *32-33*
Photomacrography, *214, 218;* and view camera, *168-169*
Picasso, Pablo, 18
Playboy magazine, 138
Pohlman Studios, *68-69;* photographs by, *69*
Poiret, Paul, 105
Polaroid back, *183, 184*
Portrait photography, 20-29; of children, *34-35;* of pets, *32-33*
Portrait studio(s): 19th Century, 46-47, *48-49;* color, *58-59;* Home of Photography, *190-196;* tintype, *50-51*

Queen magazine, 132

Rain studio, *76*
Rathe, Fred, 70
Ray, Man, 116; photographs by, *116-117*
Rayograph, 116, *117*
Reflectors, 201; and lighting technique, 204, 205, *206,* 209, 212, 230
Retouching of color photographs, 87
Revolving back, *185*
Rise and fall: definition, 144; effects of, *148-149;* and illusion of movement, 170. *See also* Movements, view camera
Rizzo, Alberto, 136; photograph by, *136*
Rockwell, George Lincoln, 16
Rogers, Roy, *59*
Room settings, photography of, *64-67*
Roosevelt, Franklin D., *23*
Roosevelt, Theodore, 22

Safelight, 179, *188*
St. John, Lynn, 230; photograph by, *230*
Sandbank, Henry, 38, 212; photographs by, *38, 212, 227*
Scheimpflug Principle, 158
Schiaparelli, Elsa, 116
Scolamiero, Peter, 38; photograph by, *39*
Seamless paper, *176-177,* 201; and lighting technique, *202-209*
Shape of image: and swing of camera-back, *154-155;* and tilt of camera-back, *152-153. See also* Distortion
Shifts: applications of, *160-161, 166-167;* definition of, 144; effects of, *150-151;* and illusion of movement, 170; and wide-field pictures, *166-167. See also* Movements, view camera
Shrimpton, Jean, 14
Siegman, Hal, *79,* 80, 81, 82
Silano, William, 134; photographs by, *134-135*
Sokolsky, Melvin, 30, 131; photographs by, *30, 131*
Spotlights, *187;* and lighting technique, 200, *203-207. See also* Lighting techniques
Steichen, Edward, *11,* 106, 110, 224; and artificial lighting, 110; photographs by, *11, 105, 110-111;* quoted, 106
Stern, Bert, 136; photographs by, *137, 226;* quoted, 130
Still-life photography, *36-37, 199, 200-201, 202-230;* of fabric, *214-215, 218;* of flowers, *222-223;* of food, *60-63, 210-211, 224-229;* of glass, *204-205, 206-207, 228-229;* of jewelry, *216-217;* lighting techniques, 200-201, *202-211;* of liquids, *219;* of metals, *208-209, 230;* of toys, *220-221;* view camera technique, *156-157;* of white objects on white backgrounds, *202-203*
Studio(s): 19th Century, *48-49;* commercial, *60-76,* 80-87; décor of, 47; early color, *58-59;* early lighting techniques of, 46, 50, 54, 56; evolution of the, 46-47, *48-60;* of Al Freni, 174-175, *176-181;* of Bob Garrett, *190-196;* on location, 88, *90-102;* movie, *54-55, 56-57;* operation of large commercial, 80-87; as team of specialists, 80-87; tintype, *50-51*
Studio, home, 174; cameras for, *182-185;* electric power for, 175; equipment for, 175, *176-179, 186-189;* layout of, *176-179;* space required for, 174-175, 180
Studio photography: characteristics of, 12-13; commercial, *36, 38-42, 47, 60-76, 80-87;* of fashion, *30-31, 105, 106-107, 108-140;* on location, 88, *90-102;* of pets, *32-33;* portraiture, *20-29, 32-35;* still-life, *36-37,* 199, *200-201, 202-230*
Studio team, 80-87; art director, 80, 82; assistant, 82; casting director, 82, 83; color retouchers, 87; copywriter, 80; display designer, 82; general manager, 81; home economists, 86; model, 80; model builder, 86; representative, 81; stylist, 80, 83-86; wardrobe mistress, 80
Stylist, varied functions of, 83-86
Swings: applications of, *162, 163;* definition of, 144; effects of, *154-155. See also* Movements, view camera

Taft, William Howard, *22*
Tanks, developing, *189*
Taylor, Elizabeth, 128
Thermometer, *188*
Tilts: definition of, 144; effects of, *152-154. See also* Movements, view camera
Timer, darkroom, *179, 188*
Tintype studio, *50-51*
Toys, photography of, *220-221*
Tree, Penelope, 14, 128, *129*
Tripods, 186
Truman, Harry S., *23*
Trutmann, B., 224; photograph by, *225*
Turner, Pete, 228; photograph by, *228*

Ungaro, Emanuel, 129

View camera(s): advantages of, 144, *184, 185;* applications, *156-170;* diagram of, *145;* equipment for, *184, 185;* and film size, *146-147;* focusing, *146,* 152, *153;* and image cutoff, 146, *165;* movements, 144, *148-155;* and photomacrography, *168-169*
Vogue magazine, 12, 16, 17, 18, 34, 98, 107, 108, 110, 112, 116, 128, 130, 138

Wakabayashi, Yesuhiro. *See* Hiro
Wantland, Henry, photograph by, *173*
Warnecke, Harry, *58-59;* photograph by, *59*
Weston, Edward, 224
Wet plate process, 47
Wetting concentrate, *188*
White, Stanford, 35
Wightman, Norman, photograph by, *33*
Wilder, Jackie, 83
Wilson, Woodrow, 22
Windsor, Duke and Duchess of, 16
Wolcott, Alexander S., studio of, 46

Ylla, photograph by, *32*

Printed in U.S.A.

XXXX